Carb-Cycling Cookbook

A Complete Guide to Reach Your Fitness Goals and Transform Your Body Without Giving Up Carbs.

Easy & Tasty Recipes Ready in 30 Minutes, Weight Loss Exercises & 30-Day Meal Plan

Kendall Anderson

Table of Contents

Chapter 1: The Basics of the Carb Cycling Diet

Understanding the basics of the carb cycling diet is the first step toward implementing it into your lifestyle.

Carb cycling is a very effective nutritional approach that involves manipulating your calorie intake by controlling your carbohydrates. This is done by limiting your calorie intake on certain days and reintroducing them into your diet on other days. Cycling your carbohydrate consumption allows your body to have periods of a calorie deficit. This, in turn, allows the body to burn stored body fat for energy and leads to weight loss.

Most endurance athletes have used carb cycling to help in optimizing energy. They do this by consuming more carbohydrates on days when they engage in intense workouts. The days on which they aren't as physically active are ones where they reduce their carbohydrate consumption significantly. These days, this diet has also become popular for those who want to lose weight.

The carb cycling diet can be adjusted according to whatever each individual's goals are. If you are not very active and your goal is to lose weight, the diet can be adjusted to meet those needs. If you are moderately active, your carbohydrates can be manipulated to meet the needs of your active days. For a very active person, like an athlete or bodybuilder, the diet is functional in a variety of ways as well. Accordingly, the carbohydrate intake of each person can be scheduled based on their goals and other factors, which are mentioned below.

- Rest days and training days—The most popular carbohydrate scheduling approach is having high-carb days when training and low-carb days when you rest.
- Body composition goal—Carbohydrates can be increased on days when you intend to work on muscle building so you can increase or maintain muscle mass. On other days, the carb count can be reduced.
- Competitions or special events—Bodybuilders or athletes who follow the diet are often known to carb-load right before an important event.
- Body fat levels—The percentage of body fat you have can also help determine how many days of low-carb or high-carb blocks you can have in your carb cycle schedule. The leaner you are, the more blocks of high or moderate-carbs consumption you can include.
- Psychological fulfillment—The psychological aspect of the diet is important because it allows you to take a break from restrictions, even when cutting down on carbs and following a diet. Other restrictive diets tend to take a negative and stressful toll on mental health.

In general, the usual weekly carb cycling plan for most people is as follows:

- Two days of high-carbohydrate consumption.
- Two days of moderate-carbohydrate consumption.
- Three days of very low-carbohydrate consumption.

It is important for every user to match their carbohydrate consumption according to their body's caloric needs. When you intend to work out intensely, it is imperative that you provide your body with an appropriate amount of carbohydrates. This allows the body to get enough glycogen, and this prevents loss of muscle mass or lack of performance abilities.

The subsequent supply of carbohydrates after low-carb days also improves hormonal function. This helps in the natural regulation of appetite and weight. During the low-carb days, your body becomes more efficient in metabolic flexibility, fat burning, and weight loss. It also improves insulin sensitivity.

Benefits of the Carb Cycling Diet

Muscle Mass Growth/Maintenance

Carb cycling is quite effective in preventing muscle loss and helps increase muscle mass when accompanied by exercise. Your body can burn fat while building muscle by alternating high-carb days with low-carb days.

Endocrine Stimulation

When you follow a low-carb diet for too long, it can lead to decreased thyroid hormone levels, which causes your basal metabolic rate to reduce too. This makes it very difficult to actually burn any fat after the initial weight loss. The carb cycling diet includes high-carb days and stabilizes thyroid hormones, thus allowing better metabolism and fat loss. The balance of low-carb days with high-carb days also allows leptin, or the "satiety hormone" levels, to remain normal. Leptin levels tend to increase a lot when you consume too many carbs for too long.

Efficient Fat Burning

When you eat fewer carbs, the body enters ketosis and burns stored fat for energy instead. The carb cycling diet allows you to tap into this particular metabolic state that then helps you efficiently burn more fat.

Improved Metabolic Flexibility

The human body is very adaptable and knows how to use carbs as well as fats for energy. However, if you continue to consume a lot of carbs consistently for a long time, it becomes less efficient in burning fats. With the carb cycling diet, the body becomes metabolically flexible and efficient again. The diet will prompt your body to burn carbs as well as fats.

Weight Loss

The diet allows you to consume carbs according to your lifestyle. This allows your body to burn calories when you exercise on a high-carb day. On days when you don't exercise, you won't be consuming too many carbs and thus won't put on weight either. With all its benefits, the diet is very helpful in losing excess weight.

You can see why the recommended carb cycling diet is becoming so popular.

Chapter 2: Difference Between Carb Cycling and the Keto Diet

A common mistake that many people make is to try combining the carb cycling diet with the keto diet because they assume that it will work more effectively. However, carb cycling, and ketogenic diets differ in many ways. It is important to pick one diet and follow the guidelines for their individual approaches to work. If you intend to follow the carb cycling diet as recommended in this book, it will help you to understand how these diets work differently.

As you now know, the carb cycling diet is a dietary approach in which you alternate your carbohydrate intake daily. You will be consuming carbohydrates but in a higher amount on some days, less on others, and sometimes maybe none at all. On the other hand, the ketogenic diet emphasizes consuming a lot of fat and the most minimal amount of carbohydrates in your diet.

Carb cycling is all about altering your carbohydrate intake according to your energy needs on different days. There is no general guideline for the exact amount since this number will vary from person to person. Previously, the diet was mostly followed by bodybuilders or professional athletes. Now, the diet is slowly becoming popular amongst others who are not as physically active. It works effectively since the diet plan can be customized according to each individual's needs. The rationale behind the diet is that the body starts burning stored fat when you limit carbohydrate consumption. You may think that this is the same as what the ketogenic diet is based on, however, they are not the same.

Following the ketogenic diet will usually consist of 60% fats, 30% proteins, and a meager 10% carbohydrates or less. The diet aims to kick your body into ketosis to burn your stored body fat. Once you start following the keto diet, your body will stay in this ketosis mode for as long as you follow the guidelines of this diet. You are told to eliminate carbs consistently for a long period.

On the other hand, the carb cycling diet allows you to alternate high-carb days with low-carb days. You won't restrict your carbohydrate intake indefinitely, and your body will not kick into ketosis unless you follow low-carb days for a longer period.

One of the main reasons that this diet works for people is that you don't have to follow a dietary plan where carbohydrates are consistently restricted. Intense diets in which you are prohibited from eating carbohydrates for long periods are not sustainable for the long term.

Most people give up on such diets and find that their weight returns when they start following their regular diet again. Carb cycling, on the other hand, allows you to consume carbs but in a more controlled way. So, even when you have a low-carb day, you will find it easy to follow the meal plan since you have a carb reload to look forward to.

It is also better than other fad diets because it doesn't cause a lot of stress on your body and mind. When you follow an intense restrictive diet, your body undergoes stress, and hormonal balance is affected too. Your weight also tends to return just as quickly as you lost it. With the carb cycling diet, your meal plan is steadier and easier to follow. The excess weight is gradually lost instead, and it doesn't cause havoc on your body.

The carb cycling diet also has another advantage over the keto diet. Reducing your carbs drastically and going on a keto or no-carb diet usually causes irritability and fatigue. These are some symptoms experienced as a part of the keto flu that people suffer from when they start following the ketogenic diet. You may also experience nausea and vomiting as part of the keto flu. These symptoms manifest because it is difficult for the body to adapt without carbs for an extended period of time. With the carb cycling diet, you only have to cut down on carbs in a very adaptable way. This allows the body to avoid such symptoms, which tend to occur as a side effect of no-carb diets.

The carb cycling diet allows you to cut down on calories without cutting out carbohydrates completely. Choosing to lower carbohydrates through this diet is a lot more feasible for someone looking for a long-term solution. Diets like the keto diet can only be followed for a certain amount of time and are not healthy or sustainable in the long-term.

Chapter 3: Shopping List, Foods to Eat, and Foods to Avoid

The carb cycling diet is easy to figure out, and you can follow a plan that works best for your needs. While following the diet, eating the right foods on the right days is the most important thing. In this section, you will find an easy-to-follow guide for your next grocery trip. You will know which foods to avoid, and which foods are appropriate for each day of your carb cycling meal plan. Remember to determine your carbohydrate consumption based on age, gender, body weight, workout intensity, and goals.

Fiber Matters

It is advised to include high-fiber carbs in your meals on low-carb days. In this way, the sense of satiety remains longer. Since carbs tend to be digested quickly most of the time, you may feel hungry soon after a low-carb meal. This is why adding more fiber to the meal can be quite helpful. It is also important to look for low-carb foods with more fiber since most of your dietary fiber comes from high-carb foods like whole grains. Fiber is also essential for cholesterol control and gut health. Flax seeds, chia seeds, broccoli, avocados, wheat bran, blackberries, coconut meat, and blackberries are foods with more fiber and low-carb content.

Quality Matters

Another important point to remember is that the quality of food you consume on this diet matters a lot. Even on high-carb days, you must pick healthy foods, not junk food.

Foods to Avoid on Carb Cycling Diet

While following the diet, opting for healthy carbs and avoiding unhealthy food is best. Processed high-carb foods will only prevent you from benefiting from the diet. Junk food provides no nutritional value to your body and only adds empty calories that are hard to lose. You need to avoid or remove the following foods from your kitchen pantry while carb cycling.

- white flour
- wheat flour
- refined sugar
- white bread
- white pasta
- sugary cereals
- sweetened drinks like sodas

Foods to Eat on Carb Cycling Diet

Eating the right foods will make all the difference while following the carb cycling diet as well as for good health in general. Avoid junk and processed food, and opt for healthy whole foods. Fresh fruits and vegetables, grass-fed meat, wild-caught fish, healthy fats like nuts, etc., should all be part of your diet. You can then prepare your meals using foods that are high, low, or moderate in carbs according to your carb cycle diet schedule.

High-Carb Days:

- raisins
- wheat tortillas
- whole grain bread
- rice
- potatoes
- bananas
- honey
- apples
- buckwheat
- amaranth
- feta cheese
- gouda cheese
- goat cheese
- whole fruits
- apricots
- pear
- pineapple
- dates
- sweet potatoes
- oats

Medium-Carb Days:

- milk
- beans
- tomatoes
- mushrooms
- sea veggies
- pepper
- natural yogurt
- cheese
- vegetable juice
- corn
- quinoa
- yogurt
- beetroot
- legumes
- peanut butter
- blueberries
- raspberries
- blackberries

Low-Carb Days:

- salmon
- asparagus
- broccoli
- seeds
- walnuts
- pine nuts
- tofu
- radishes
- fresh dill
- trout
- cage-free eggs
- Brussels sprouts
- beef
- chicken
- pork
- cucumbers

- chicory
- cauliflower
- organ meats
- raw goat cheese
- coconut oil
- extra virgin olive oil

Spices For Any Day:

- red paprika
- yellow paprika
- green paprika
- oregano
- basil
- balsamic vinegar
- rosemary
- thyme
- soy sauce
- cinnamon
- salt
- dried marjoram
- nutmeg
- baking powder
- mustard
- baking soda
- cayenne pepper

The foods you need to consume should also be based on your goals. Do you want to focus on losing weight with the carb cycling diet first? Is your goal to use the carb cycling diet to supplement your muscle-building endeavors? Considering these, you will be able to determine the right foods to help you reach your goals faster. For instance, high-protein foods are better for you when you want to build or maintain muscle. When you want to lose weight, lower the amount of fat you consume and always opt for healthy fats.

Foods that fuel your muscle-building goals include salmon, tuna, Greek yogurt, milk, chicken, eggs, nuts and seeds, avocados, oatmeal, and chickpeas.

Foods that will help you reach your goal weight include leafy greens, apples, asparagus, fish, eggs, bell peppers, lentils, berries, broccoli, chia seeds, etc.

You can check any food's calories and overall macronutrients to make better meal choices.

Among beverages, consuming coffee and tea without any sugar or cream on any day is safe. More importantly, remember to hydrate often, especially on low-carb days when you feel dizzy. A lot of the time, you will also find that you mistake thirst for hunger, and you can curb this by drinking a glass of water. A well-hydrated body is key to staying healthy alongside your diet.

Chapter 4: Weight Loss Exercises for Home Workout

Exercising is a crucial part of following the carb cycling diet. While athletes and bodybuilders already have their own workouts when using this diet, you also need to start doing some regular exercises. However, starting with some easy movements is best if you never work out in general. This section includes instructions for numerous exercises for beginners, intermediates, and experts. You can start with beginner exercises and work your way to the expert movements. The more weight you lose and muscle mass you build, the easier it will be to become more flexible and stronger.

Exercises for Beginners

If you are not active and have a lot of weight to lose, it is best not to start with intensive exercises. Begin with stretches and easy workouts to help you loosen your muscles, increase flexibility, and build stamina. Some exercises are simple and very effective in helping beginners lose weight. You can try any of the following and implement them into your daily routine in addition to carb cycling.

Bent Over Twist

The bent over twist is one of the simplest exercises but is an essential part of a warm-up for beginners. It helps in improving stability and flexibility. It helps you work primarily on your obliques but also on your abs, hamstrings, and lower back.

1. Stand straight maintaining a shoulder-width distance between your feet. Raise your arms to your sides at shoulder height.

2. Now bend your torso and rotate it downwards to the right. Touch your right foot with your left hand. Engage your abs and control your movement with your obliques. Breathe out as you do this.
3. Move back up to the initial position as you breathe in.
4. Then repeat the same exercise with the other side of your body.
5. Do 15 repetitions on each side as a warm-up for any workout routine.

Knee Push-up

This exercise is easier than a regular push-up since it requires less upper-body strength.

1. Get down on the floor with your knees touching the ground. Your hands should be shoulder width apart. Keep your knees crossed and above. Your torso, hips, and head should be in line.
2. Keep your back straight and bend your elbows to lower your body to the ground. Try to bring your chest as close to the ground as possible. Inhale while you bring yourself down.
3. Pause for a second in that position and then push your body back up to the first position. Exhale as you come up.
4. Repeat and do as many reps as possible and increase them daily. Ultimately, you should soon be able to do at least 20-25 reps.

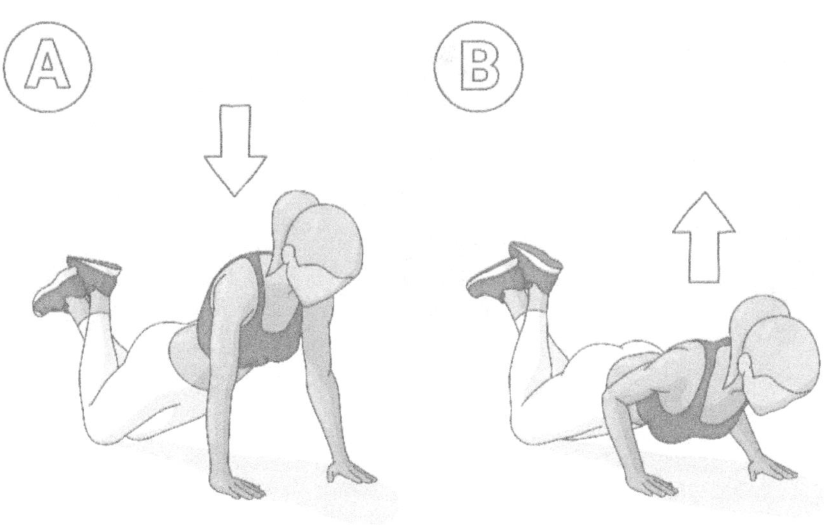

Bicep Curls

Bicep curls help sculpt the upper body and tone your biceps and shoulders. It is also a good arm-strengthening exercise.

1. Stand straight with your feet apart and hold a dumbbell in each hand. Keep your hands by your sides, facing outward. Keep your head up and back straight.
2. Pull your shoulders back and straight. Now squeeze your biceps and lift your forearms with the dumbbells. Keep upper arms stationary and elbows close to the body. While lifting the weights, exhale.
3. After you pull the dumbbells up to shoulder level, take a pause and slowly lower them back down. As you lower the weights, inhale
4. Repeat and do 10 reps of this exercise to build up to two sets with time.

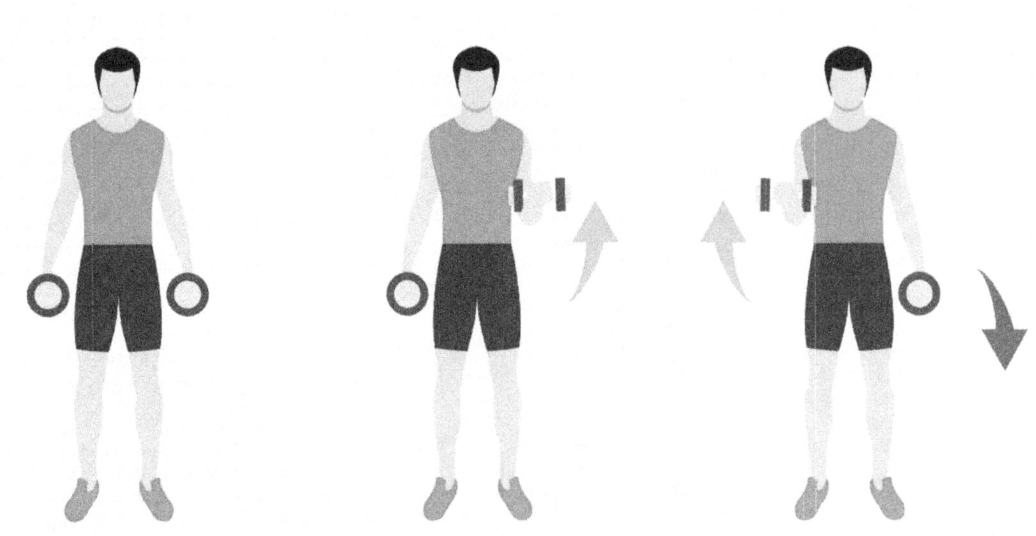

Side Lunge

Side lunges are great for working on your inner thighs, quads, glutes, and hamstrings. This is a lateral movement that will benefit your inner and outer thighs both while toning that area. It is a complete exercise that helps you strengthen your lower body.

1. Keep your body straight with a hip wide distance between your feet. Hold your hands up to your side as you get ready.
2. Now step out to one side and transfer your weight to that leg as you squat it slightly. Your back should be straight, and your abs should be pulled in. Breathe in while stepping out, and ensure your knees are pointed in the same direction as your feet. Bring your hands to the center of your body together to help maintain balance.
3. Using your lead foot, return to your starting position. Breathe out while you do this.
4. Switch to the other side and repeat the side lunge.
5. Do 10 reps on each side and work your way to completing two sets of this.

Cross Crunches

Cross crunches engage your oblique muscles and abs. They help in sculpting your waist and burn abdominal fat. You will also be strengthening your core and toning the torso.

1. Lie on your back and bend your knees.
2. Support the back of your head with your left hand and cross the opposite right leg over your left knee.
3. Make your abs work as you crunch, and bring your left elbow toward your right knee. Breathe out while doing this.
4. Breathe in and bring your body back to the initial position.
5. Repeat these cross crunches on one side 10 times and switch to the other side for 10 more reps.
6. Work your way to doing 2 sets of 10 reps each during every workout.

Butterfly Stretch

The butterfly stretch engages your inner thighs, hip flexors, and hamstrings. It helps in opening up your thighs and hips. This improves your lower body flexibility and stretches the adductors. These muscles are usually neglected but they serve an important role in balance. The butterfly stretch will also improve your mobility and posture.

1. Sit down on the ground and bring both your feet toward each other and inwards toward your body. Straighten your back and push your shoulders back.
2. Use your hands to hold and slightly push your knees into the floor. Keep your core tight. Breathe out while you do this.
3. Hold your position for 20 seconds and then release. Breathe in as you return to the initial position.
4. Do this stretch every time you do a lower body workout to further stretch the muscles in that region.

Exercises for Intermediates

If you are slightly active and like to do some form of exercise once in a while, you can try these intermediate-level exercises. They will help you achieve your weight loss goals, build or maintain muscle and allow you to increase your strength.

Regular Push-up

Push-ups are a great upper body exercise that strengthens your core, increases upper body strength, and improves metabolic rate too.

1. Get down on your hands and legs. Keep your hands a little wider than the width of your shoulders.
2. Keep your legs and arms straight.
3. Now lower your whole body until you can almost touch the floor with your chest.
4. Pause for a second, and then push yourself up on all fours again.
5. Repeat and do as many reps as you can when you first start working out. Work your way to 20 reps in three sets over time.

Squat

Squats are a bodyweight exercise that is low in intensity but can be very effective. They help in toning your glutes and legs. It will also help in strengthening the muscles in your knees. You will see that your overall body balance and flexibility improve with squats.

1. Stand with your feet parallel to your shoulder. Keep your hands to your sides. Your back should be in alignment, and your chest should be up while your hips are back.
2. First, bend your knees while pressing your hips back, and make sure that your knees don't extend beyond your toes. Breathe in as you squat down and pause when your hips go a little lower than your knees.
3. Press your heels into the ground and push yourself back to the initial position. Breathe out as you do this.
4. Repeat and try to do 15 reps of this to build your way to three sets over time.

Donkey Kicks

Donkey kicks are great for working on your abs, hip flexors, and glutes. This exercise will tighten and tone your buttocks while strengthening your core.

1. Get down on the ground on all fours. Put your hands equally spaced under your shoulders and your knees directly beneath your hips.
2. Stand straight and keep your core tight. Face downwards and breathe out as you kick one leg back while squeezing the glutes. Make sure not to raise that backward leg higher than your hips.
3. Bend that knee and lower it back down. Breathe in while you do this.
4. Switch the leg and repeat the exercise. Repeat it 15 times on each leg and work your way to three sets of this over time.

Bicycle Crunches

Bicycle crunches are great if you want to slim down your waist and increase strength in your core. It is also a good flexibility and stability exercise. Your heart rate is boosted, and your metabolic rate improves too. It works primarily on your abs, obliques, hip flexors, quads, and glutes.

1. Lie down on your back and keep your neck relaxed. Lift your shoulders and place your hands behind your head. Your elbows should be open.
2. Bring one knee toward the opposite elbow as you move it forward by crunching toward that side. Extend the other leg. Engage your core as you do this.
3. Get back to the relaxed position and do the entire exercise with your other leg and elbow. Maintain a steady rhythm.
4. Repeat this exercise with both legs about 12-15 times and work toward three sets when you work out.

Downward Dog Crunch

A downward dog crunch works on multiple muscles since it is a full body-engaging exercise. It helps to tighten your core, improve your spinal posture, and improve your overall strength. It also elevates your heart rate and allows for faster fat burning. The downward dog pose is great for removing stress and elongating your body. It helps eliminate any stiffness and invigorates your body.

1. Start by getting into the plank pose. Rest your hands on the ground at a shoulder-width distance.
2. Keep your hands and feet planted while you lift your hips upwards and backward. This is the downward dog pose. Remove any tension from your neck, and keep your elbows straight. Press down with your fingers spread and straighten your knees.
3. Once you are in the downward dog pose, bring the right knee toward your right elbow as you crunch. Breathe in while doing this. Engage your core and maintain the rest of your position.
4. Breathe in and extend your right leg back and up from the bent knee crunch. Remember not to arch your back while doing this.
5. Repeat this movement on the right side 10 times.
6. Return to the downward dog pose and repeat the crunch with your left leg 10 times.
7. Do at least 10 reps for each side with two-three sets.

Pilates Swimming

The pilates swimming movement engages your entire back and core. It strengthens the muscles and tones your core. Your mobility and posture will both improve. The movement also improves overall body alignment.

1. Lie down on the ground with your belly down. Fully extend your legs and arms while maintaining a neutral spine. Try to elongate your body without straining it.
2. Raise your elongated arms and legs as you lift your chest and head off the mat. Maintain stability in your upper body and hips when you start this exercise.
3. Pull your abs tight and move your right leg upwards simultaneously with your left hand. Bring both down and flutter the left leg upwards with your right hand. Keep alternating and continue the movement without placing your hands and legs down.

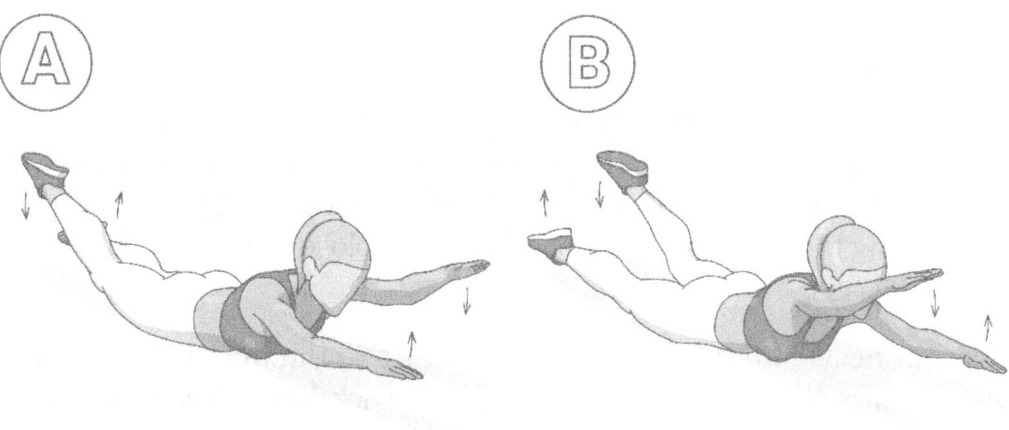

Exercises for Experts

Athletes, bodybuilders, and anyone who is active regularly can try all kinds of different exercises since their body is prepared for them. Certain exercises can be too exertive for beginners but are not too difficult for experts. Beginner exercises may also not be as effective for experts since their body is already conditioned for such exercises.

Squats With Dumbbells

Squats are a great bodyweight exercise and even better with dumbbells. This exercise will help to tone your glutes and legs while building muscle mass. It will increase body strength and help burn fat, especially in your core.

1. Stand straight and keep your legs at ease. Hold a dumbbell in each hand with your palms facing forward. Your back should align, and your chest should be up while your hips are back.
2. Now bend your knees while pressing your hips back, and ensure your knees don't extend beyond your toes. Breathe in as you squat down and pause when your hips go slightly lower than your knees. While bending down, curl your forearms upwards while holding the dumbbells. Keep your elbows close to your body, and don't move your upper arms.
3. Press your heels into the ground and stand up to the initial position. Uncurl your biceps as you come up and bring the dumbbells back down. Breathe out as you do this.
4. Repeat and try to do 10 reps of this to build your way to three sets over time.

Dumbbell Triceps Kickback

The dumbbell triceps kickback works primarily on your triceps but also helps to tone your arms. It is good for burning body fat and increases your upper body strength.

1. Stand with your knees slightly bent and bring your torso bending forward. Keep your back straight and not curved. Keep your head in line with your spine and engage your core.
2. Pull your forearms up with the dumbbells in your hands while bending your elbows. Keep the upper arm parallel to the ground. Kick your hands back till they are fully extended backward. Exhale as you kick back.
3. Now slowly bend your elbows and bring your weights back to the initial position.
4. Repeat this eight-ten times and work your way to four sets of this exercise. Increase the weight of the dumbbells when you find it too easy.

Cobra Lat Pulldown

The cobra lat pulldown allows you to work on your lower back, lats, chest, and upper back. It strengthens the muscles in your back and helps to keep your spine in alignment. If you have bad posture, this exercise can help fix it and can also help prevent related lower back pain.

1. Lie down on your stomach and then extend your legs and arms completely. Your head should be aligned to your spine. Avoid straining your neck while doing the exercise. Your arms and legs should be extended away from your body.
2. Breathe out and bend your arms inwards as you raise your upper body. Keep your shoulders away from your ears. Your legs should be pulled together.
3. Take a breath and lower your upper body while extending your arms outward again. Extend your legs outward into the original position.

Boat Twist

Boat twist works primarily on your obliques, abs, and lower back. It engages your entire core region and is a strengthening exercise. It helps in slimming your waist and burns fat in your hips. It also improves your stability and balance.

1. Sit down and bend your knees a little. Set your arms parallel to the ground and out to the sides. Lift your feet off the ground. This is the starting position.
2. Now breathe out and twist your torso to the right with your arms extended and feet off the floor. Your back should remain straight the entire time.
3. Reverse the motion and twist your torso to the left.
4. Repeat the movement from left to right without putting your feet back on the ground. Do 10 twists and take a break before repeating another set.

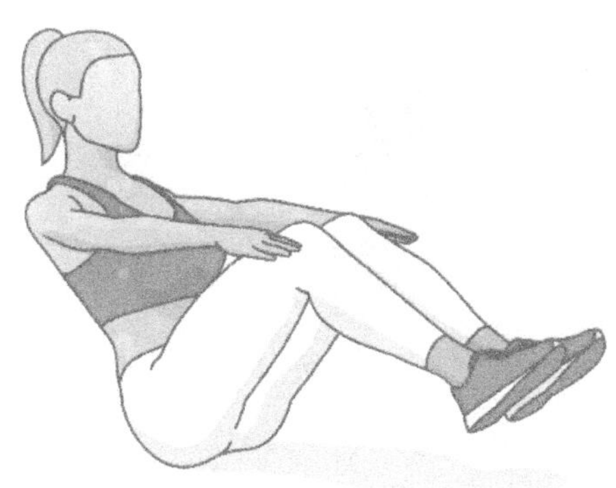

Bent Leg Jackknife

The bent leg jackknife engages your abs, hip flexors, core, upper back, and quads. It strengthens your core and helps in tightening the muscles there. It improves back posture and helps prevent lower back pain.

1. Lie down on the mat. Extend your arms backward and keep your legs extended straight downwards.
2. Raise your torso upwards. Bend and bring your knees toward your chest as you breathe out. While doing this exercise, contract your abs.
3. Return back to the initial position as you breathe in. Keep your hands and feet off the ground and repeat the motion.
4. Repeat this 10 times and do two sets.

Butterfly Dips

Butterfly dips engage your triceps, shoulders, chest, glutes, and inner thighs. This exercise is a version of the tricep dip exercise. It strengthens your triceps, inner thighs, and upper body. It also sculpts your glutes.

1. Sit on the ground and slightly bend your knees while bringing your feet together. Keep your hands behind and a bit more than shoulder width apart. Keep your fingers pointing forward and your thighs open.
2. Breathe out, press down with your hands, and push your arms straight up while also pressing your hips upwards. Bring your thighs and knees together as you do this. Pause in this position.
3. Inhale, bend your elbows and return to the initial position.
4. Repeat this movement 10 times and work your way to three sets.

Tips to Make Carb Cycling More Effective

- Don't make drastic changes to your diet right away. You need to pace yourself and only take on as much as you can handle. Make a few small changes in your diet first, then switch to a full-fledged carb cycling diet.
- Taking health supplements while trying this diet might help boost your metabolism and maintain digestive health. Probiotics are known to improve digestion and gut health. Omega-3 fatty acids will fight inflammation. If you work out a lot, magnesium supplements will help support recovery. Multivitamins will ensure that you get the recommended daily amount of vitamins your body needs. And, if you struggle with stress, you may also want to try an adaptogen herb.

Chapter 5: Breakfast Recipes

Veggie Scrambled Eggs

Level: Easy
Carbs: Low
Serves: 3
Preparation time: 5-6 minutes
Cooking time: 10-12 minutes

Ingredients:

- *2 tablespoons olive oil*
- *⅛ cup chopped onions*
- *3 eggs*
- *⅛ cup chopped fresh tomato*
- *⅛ cup sliced fresh mushrooms*
- *⅛ cup chopped green bell peppers*
- *⅛ cup shredded cheddar cheese*
- *⅛ cup milk*
- *salt and pepper to taste*

Directions:

1. Place a pan over medium-high heat. Add the olive oil and let it heat. Once the oil is hot, drop the onion, mushrooms, and bell pepper into the pan and stir.
2. Meanwhile, crack the eggs into a bowl. Add the milk and seasonings and beat well.
3. Pour the eggs into the pan and add the tomatoes. Mix well. Add the cheese and whisk when the eggs are almost set.
4. Serve.

Nutritional value per serving: Calories: 182, Fat: 15.6 g, Carbohydrates: 2.1 g, Sugar: 2 g, Protein: 8.2 g

Spinach Enchilada Omelet

Level: Easy
Serves: 3
Preparation time: 10 minutes

Carbs: Low
Cooking time: 20-25 minutes

Ingredients:

- *¾ cup shredded Colby Jack cheese*
- *½ cup enchilada sauce*
- *5 ounces of frozen spinach*
- *¼ cup green onions plus extra to garnish*
- *½ can (from a 4.5-ounce can) of chopped green chilies*
- *½ avocado, diced*
- *salt and pepper to taste*
- *1 tablespoon chopped fresh cilantro plus extra to garnish*
- *1 ½ cups egg whites*
- *½ teaspoon extra-virgin olive oil*
- *cooking spray*
- *½ medium tomato, diced*
- *1 tablespoon water*

Directions:

1. Preheat the oven to 350 °F.
2. Spread 3 tablespoons of enchilada sauce on the bottom of a baking dish.
3. Add the egg whites, seasonings, and water into a bowl and whisk until they are well combined.
4. To make the egg tortillas: Place a medium-sized non-stick skillet over medium heat. Spray with cooking spray.
5. Pour about ⅓ of the egg whites (about ½ cup) into the hot pan. To spread the whites out, swirl the pan. Cook for about a minute or until it sets. Flip to the other side and cook for 40-60 seconds when the tortilla is set. Slide the tortilla onto a plate.
6. Repeat the process with the remaining egg whites and make the other two tortillas.
7. Heat olive oil in a pan. Add the green onion and cook for a couple of minutes.
8. Stir in the tomato, cilantro, and salt, and cook for about a minute.
9. Add the spinach and green chili. Cook until the spinach turns limp.
10. Add seasonings. Turn off the heat. Add ¼ cup cheese and stir.
11. Divide the vegetable mixture among the tortillas.
12. Roll and place in the baking dish, with the seam side touching the bottom of the dish.
13. Spread the remaining sauce and cheese over the rolls.
14. Cover the baking dish with foil, place it in the oven, and bake for 15-20 minutes.
15. Sprinkle green onions and avocado on top and serve.

Nutritional value per serving: Calories: 281, Fat: 16.1 g, Carbohydrates: 13.4 g, Sugar: 2.8 g, Protein: 22.9 g

Smoked Salmon and Cream Cheese Omelet

Level: Easy
Serves: 2
Preparation time: 15 minutes

Carbs: Low

Cooking time: 15 minutes

Ingredients:

- *4 large eggs*
- *salt and pepper to taste*
- *2 teaspoons butter*
- *⅛ cup crumbled feta or cream cheese, softened*
- *3 teaspoons chopped fresh dill plus extra to garnish*
- *2 teaspoons water*
- *¼ cup chopped smoked salmon*
- *⅛ cup finely chopped red onion*

Directions:

1. Add the water and seasoning to a bowl, break the eggs in it and beat it all well.
2. Add 1 teaspoon of butter into a small skillet and let it melt over medium-low heat. Swirl the pan to spread butter.
3. Pour in half of the egg mixture and cook the omelet for about a minute. Scatter half of each—salmon, onion, cheese, and dill on one half of the omelet. Let it cook for about a minute or until the omelet is almost set.
4. Fold the omelet. Continue cooking for a minute. Turn the omelet over and cook the other side for a minute. Transfer onto a plate. Garnish with dill and serve.
5. Similarly, make the other omelet (steps 2-4).

Nutritional value per serving: Calories: 254, Fat: 19.2 g, Carbohydrates: 2.3 g, Sugar: 2 g, Protein: 16.7 g

Omelet Muffins

Level: Easy
Serves: 3
Preparation time: 10 minutes

Carbs: Low

Cooking time: 25 minutes

Ingredients:

- *1 ½ slices bacon, chopped*
- *2 scallions, sliced*
- *½ cup shredded cheddar cheese*
- *¼ teaspoon salt*
- *1 cup finely chopped broccoli*
- *4 large eggs*
- *¼ cup low-fat milk*
- *¼ teaspoon pepper*

Directions:

1. Preheat the oven to 350 °F. Grease a 6-count muffin pan with cooking oil spray.
2. Meanwhile, add the bacon to a pan and place it over medium heat. Cook until crispy.

3. Take out the bacon with the help of a slotted spoon and place it over paper towels to drain.
4. Add the scallions and bacon into the pan with the bacon drippings and cook until tender. Take it off the heat and cool for 5 minutes.
5. Add the milk, seasonings, and eggs in a bowl and beat the mixture. Add the cheese, broccoli, and bacon, and stir.
6. Distribute the broccoli mixture into the muffin pan and place it in the oven. Bake until it sets, it should roughly take 25 minutes. Cool for 5 minutes in the pan itself. Remove from the pan and serve.

Nutritional value per serving: Calories: 212, Fat: 15.5 g, Carbohydrates: 5.2 g, Sugar: 2.1 g, Protein: 16 g

Parmesan Spinach Cakes

Level: Easy
Serves: 8
Preparation time: 10 minutes
Carbs: Low
Cooking time: 15 minutes

Ingredients:

- *24 ounces fresh spinach, finely chopped*
- *1 cup finely shredded parmesan cheese plus extra to garnish*
- *2 cloves garlic, minced*
- *½ teaspoon freshly ground pepper*
- *1 cup part-skim ricotta cheese or low-fat cottage cheese*
- *4 large eggs, beaten*
- *½ teaspoon salt*

Directions:

1. You can chop the spinach in the food processor in batches.
2. Preheat the oven to 400 °F. Grease eight cups of a 12-count muffin pan with cooking oil spray.
3. Combine the spinach, parmesan, ricotta, garlic, eggs, and seasonings in a bowl.
4. Distribute the spinach mixture among the muffin cups. The cups will be full.
5. Place the muffin pan in the oven and bake until firm. Cool for about 5 minutes in the pan itself.
6. Run a knife around the edges of the muffins and invert onto a plate.

Nutritional value per serving: Calories: 141, Fat: 7.8 g, Carbohydrates: 5.6 g, Sugar: 1 g, Protein: 13.2 g

Yogurt Pancakes

Level: Easy
Serves: 1
Preparation time: 5 minutes
Carbs: Low
Cooking time: 3-4 minutes

Ingredients:

- *1 ½ teaspoons coconut flour*
- *3 tablespoons almond flour*
- *2 tablespoons plain Greek yogurt*
- *pinch of baking powder*
- *⅛ teaspoon vanilla extract*
- *1 ½ tablespoons egg whites*

Directions:

1. Add all the dry ingredients into a bowl to make the batter, i.e., coconut flour, almond flour, and baking powder. Mix well.
2. Add the Greek yogurt, vanilla extract, and egg whites and whisk until well incorporated.
3. Heat a non-stick pan over medium. Wait for the pan to heat up.
4. Spoon the batter into the pan. Spread it slightly. Now cover the pan with a lid.
5. Let it cook for a few minutes (about 2-3 minutes) until the underside is golden brown.
6. Cook the pancake on both sides.
7. The pancake is now ready to serve. Use your favorite toppings.

Nutritional value per serving: Calories: 146.2, Fat: 10.3 g, Carbohydrates: 6.7 g, Sugar: 2 g, Protein: 9 g

---

Veggie Hash

Level: Easy
Serves: 2
Preparation time: 10 minutes
Carbs: Low
Cooking time: 20-25 minutes

Ingredients:

- *1 tablespoon olive oil*
- *½ cup trimmed, halved Brussels sprouts*
- *⅛ cup diced onion*
- *⅛ teaspoon paprika*
- *2 large eggs*
- *½ enormous turnip, peeled, diced*
- *½ cup sliced asparagus*
- *1 teaspoon minced garlic*
- *⅛ teaspoon chili powder*
- *salt and pepper to taste*

Directions:

1. Add oil into a small skillet and place it over medium heat.
2. Once the oil is hot, drop the Brussels sprouts and turnip into the pan and stir.
3. Stir often until the vegetables are slightly tender and brown as well.

4. Stir in the garlic and seasonings. Keep stirring for a few seconds until you get a pleasant aroma, making sure not to burn the spices.
5. Make 2 cavities at different spots in the vegetable mixture. Crack an egg into each cavity. Sprinkle salt and pepper over the eggs and cook the eggs as per your preference.

Nutritional value per serving: Calories: 171, Fat: 12 g, Carbohydrates: 8.9 g, Sugar: 3.3 g, Protein: 8.9 g

Avocado Egg Tarts

Level: Easy
Carbs: Low
Serves: 2
Preparation time: 5 minutes
Cooking time: 20 minutes

Ingredients:

- *1 avocado, halved lengthwise, pitted*
- *2 large eggs*
- *salt and pepper to taste*

Directions:

1. Do not peel the avocados.
2. Preheat the oven to 425 °F.
3. Put the avocado halves in a baking dish with the skin side down.
4. In each avocado cavity, crack an egg. Place the baking dish in the oven and bake until the eggs are cooked, as per your preference. Sprinkle salt and pepper on top.

Nutritional value per serving: Calories: 223, Fat: 18 g, Carbohydrates: 8 g, Sugar: 0.7 g, Protein: 7 g

Egg Muffin Cups

Level: Easy
Carbs: Low
Serves: 6
Preparation time: 10 minutes
Cooking time: 15 minutes

Ingredients:

- *½ tablespoon olive oil*
- *½ cup diced green bell pepper*
- *½ cup diced red bell pepper*
- *1 cup packed baby spinach, roughly chopped*
- *1 clove garlic, minced*
- *½ cup diced onion*
- *½ cup diced mushrooms*
- *2 large egg whites*
- *2 large eggs*
- *salt to taste*
- *hot sauce to serve*

Directions:

1. Preheat the oven to 425 °F. Coat a 6-count muffin pan with a generous amount of oil or use cooking spray.
2. Over medium heat, heat a nonstick pan. Pour oil into the pan and wait for it to heat.
3. Add the onion and the bell peppers into the hot oil and stir. Stir often until the veggies are tender.
4. Stir in the mushrooms and spinach and cook for a couple of minutes.
5. Add the garlic and mix well. Cook for about 30 seconds, stirring often.
6. Turn off the heat and add salt to taste. Let it cool for 5-7 minutes.
7. Combine the eggs and egg whites in a bowl and whisk well.
8. Add the sautéed vegetables and stir.
9. Divide the mixture into the muffin pan. Place the muffin pan in the oven and bake until the eggs are set (for about 20 minutes).
10. Cool and drizzle hot sauce on top and serve.

Nutritional value per serving: Calories: 52, Fat: 2.3 g, Carbohydrates: 3.2 g, Sugar: 0.8 g, Protein: 5.4 g

---

MODERATE-CARB RECIPES

Bagel Avocado Toast

Level: Easy
Serves: 2
Preparation time: 5 minutes
Carbs: Moderate
Cooking time: 2-3 minutes

Ingredients:

- *½ medium avocado, peeled, mashed*
- *4 teaspoons of Everything bagel seasoning*
- *2 slices whole-grain bread*
- *flake sea salt to garnish*

Directions:

1. Toast the bread slices to the desired crispiness. Smear the mashed avocado on the bread slices.
2. Sprinkle 2 teaspoons of seasoning on each toast. Garnish with salt and serve.

Nutritional value per serving: Calories: 171, Fat: 10.9 g, Carbohydrates: 17 g, Sugar: 2 g, Protein: 5.2 g

---

Cottage Cheese Bowl

Level: Easy
Serves: 2

Carbs: Moderate
Preparation time: 5 minutes

Ingredients:

For the sweet bowl:

- *1 cup cottage cheese*
- *¼ cup chopped walnuts*
- *½ teaspoon ground cinnamon or more to taste*
- *¼ cup chopped almonds*
- *½ cup blueberries*

For the savory bowl:

- *1 cup cottage cheese*
- *½ cup grape tomatoes, sliced*
- *⅛ cup chopped chives or more to taste*
- *½ cup sliced cucumber*
- *1 avocado, peeled, sliced*

Directions:

1. Make any bowl of your choice—sweet or savory.
2. For a sweet bowl: Combine the cottage cheese, walnuts, almonds, and blueberries. Distribute into two bowls. Garnish with cinnamon and serve.
3. For the savory bowl: Divide the cream cheese into two bowls. Divide equally the tomatoes, cucumber, and avocado among the bowls. Garnish with chives and serve.

Nutritional value per serving: Calories: 371, Fat: 28 g, Carbohydrates: 16 g, Sugar: 8 g, Protein: 19 g

Yogurt Bowl

Level: Easy
Serves: 2

Carbs: Moderate
Preparation time: 10 minutes

Ingredients:

- *1 cup mixed berries*
- *6 tablespoons granola*
- *1 ½ cups honey vanilla Greek yogurt*
- *2 teaspoons chia seeds*
- *¼ cup sliced nuts of your choice*

Directions:

1. Take two bowls and place ¾ cup of yogurt in each.
2. Place ½ cup of the berries in each bowl, followed by 3 tablespoons of the granola and half the nuts. Sprinkle chia seeds on top and serve.

Nutritional value per serving: Calories: 206, Fat: 7 g, Carbohydrates: 21.3 g, Sugar: 13.4 g, Protein: 16.4 g

Southwest Tortilla Scramble

Level: Easy
Serves: 1
Preparation time: 5 minutes

Carbs: Moderate
Cooking time: 10 minutes

Ingredients:

- *1 large egg*
- *2 large egg whites*
- *pepper to taste*
- *⅛ cup chopped fresh spinach leaves*
- *⅛ cup salsa*
- *1 corn tortilla (6 inches), halved, cut into strips*
- *1 tablespoon shredded low-fat cheddar cheese*

Directions:

1. Add the egg, egg whites, and pepper into a bowl and whisk until well combined.
2. Add the spinach, tortilla, and cheese and mix well.
3. Heat a skillet over medium heat, and spray some cooking spray on it.
4. Add the tortilla mixture and stir often until the eggs are cooked.
5. Spoon the salsa on top and serve.

Nutritional value per serving: Calories: 194, Fat: 7 g, Carbohydrates: 16 g, Sugar: 2.2 g, Protein: 17 g

Vegan Superfood Breakfast Bowl

Level: Easy
Serves: 2
Preparation time: 10 minutes

Carbs: Moderate
Cooking time: 0 minutes plus chilling time

Ingredients:

- *2 cups of plant-based milk of your choice*
- *4 tablespoons chia seeds*
- *4 tablespoons coconut flakes*
- *⅛ cup chopped walnuts*
- *⅛ cup chopped pecans*
- *½ cup plant-based protein powder (naturally sweetened)*
- *1 tablespoon hemp seeds*
- *¼ cup mixed berries*

Directions:

1. Combine the milk, chia seeds, protein powder, coconut, and hemp seeds in a bowl.
2. Keep the bowl covered in the refrigerator all night.
3. The following morning, stir in the nuts and berries.
4. Divide the mixture into two bowls and serve.

Nutritional value per serving: Calories: 503, Fat: 37 g, Carbohydrates: 19 g, Sugar: 4.3 g, Protein: 32 g

Oatmeal with Cheddar, Collards, and Eggs

Level: Easy
Serves: 2
Preparation time: 15 minutes

Carbs: Moderate

Cooking time: 15 – 20 minutes

Ingredients:

- *1 cup rolled oats*
- *¼ teaspoon salt, divided*
- *3 teaspoons extra-virgin olive oil, divided*
- *¼ teaspoon pepper, divided*
- *1 tablespoon finely chopped shallot*
- *1 ¼ cups of water*
- *½ cup shredded cheddar cheese*
- *5 cups chopped collard greens*
- *2 large eggs*
- *1 teaspoon red wine vinegar*
- *⅛ cup chipotle salsa plus extra to serve*

Directions:

1. Add 1 ½ teaspoons of olive oil into a saucepan and place the pan over medium-high heat. Once the oil is hot, add the shallots and cook for a few minutes until they are brown.
2. Stir in the oats. Stir often for about a minute, until lightly toasted. Pour 2 cups of water, half the salt and pepper, and stir. When it starts boiling, turn down the heat and simmer until the oats are well cooked. Stir occasionally. Turn off the heat.
3. Add cheese and salsa and stir and mix everything well.
4. While the oats are cooking, place a non-stick pan over medium heat. Add remaining olive oil to the pan. When the oil is hot, add the remaining water and collards. Add the remaining salt and pepper and mix well. Cook until the collard chard is tender. Turn off the heat and add vinegar and mix well.
5. Divide the cooked oats into two bowls. Divide the collard greens equally and place them over the oats.
6. Cook the eggs as you prefer. The best options are boiled, poached, or sunny side up; sprinkle some salt and pepper over the eggs.
7. Place an egg in each bowl and serve with some extra salsa.

Nutritional value per serving: Calories: 436, Fat: 24.5 g, Carbohydrates: 33 g, Protein: 21 g

Breakfast Burrito

Level: Easy
Serves: 2
Preparation time: 10 minutes
Carbs: Moderate
Cooking time: 8 minutes

Ingredients:

- *1 egg*
- *½ tablespoon cream cheese*
- *½ clove garlic, grated*
- *⅛ large avocado, peeled, sliced*
- *1 heaping tablespoon of mozzarella cheese*
- *1 small corn tortilla (about 6 inches)*
- *½ jalapeño, sliced*
- *½ tablespoon tomato paste*
- *handful of spinach, chopped*
- *½ scallion, thinly sliced*
- *1 teaspoon olive oil*

Directions:

1. Heat a nonstick pan on medium heat. Crack the egg into the pan and stir often until the egg is soft-cooked. Turn off the heat.
2. Add the tomato paste, garlic, cream cheese, and ½ teaspoon of olive oil into a bowl and stir.
3. Spread the tomato paste mixture all over the tortilla, leaving the border.
4. Place the scrambled egg, avocado, cheese, spinach, and scallion on the tortilla. Fold into a burrito.
5. Clean the pan and place it over medium-high heat. Brush the remaining oil over the burrito and place it in the pan. Cook the burrito until golden brown on each side.
6. Serve hot.

Nutritional value per serving: Calories: 401, Fat: 27.8 g, Carbohydrates: 21 g, Sugar: 3.2 g, Protein: 16 g

Berry Yogurt Breakfast Parfait

Level: Easy
Serves: 2
Carbs: Moderate
Preparation time: 5 minutes

Ingredients:

- *2 cups vanilla Greek yogurt*
- *1 cup raspberries*
- *1 cup blueberries*
- *1 cup chopped strawberries*
- *½ cup pecans*
- *½ cup granola*

Directions:

1. Take two parfait glasses or mason jars and place ½ cup yogurt each.
2. Layer with half of each berry in any colorful manner you desire.
3. Divide half the granola and pecans equally and place them in the glasses.

4. Repeat the layers (yogurt, berries, granola, and pecans).
5. Chill until ready to serve. If the yogurt and berries are chilled, you can serve them immediately. It tastes great, as the granola will be crunchy if served immediately.
6. You can also fill the glasses with layers of only yogurt and berries and chill until ready to serve. Top with granola and pecans just before serving.

Nutritional value per serving: Calories: 258.3, Fat: 13.5 g, Carbohydrates: 29.3 g, Sugar: 16, Protein: 8.3 g

Banana Waffles

Level: Easy
Carbs: Moderate
Number of servings: 2
Preparation time: 5-8 minutes
Cooking time: 10 minutes
Total time: 15-18 minutes

Ingredients:

- *½ cup rolled oats*
- *1 egg*
- *1 medium ripe banana, peeled, chopped*
- *½ teaspoon vanilla extract*
- *½ teaspoon baking powder*
- *a pinch of salt*

Directions:

1. Add the banana, oats, egg, baking powder, salt and vanilla into a blender. Blend until the batter is lump-free and completely smooth.
2. Read the manufacturer's instructions and preheat the waffle maker and spray cooking oil on it.
3. Use 1/2 the batter and pour into the waffle maker. Cook for 3-5 minutes with the lid closed.
4. Remove the waffle from the waffle maker and serve with any toppings of your choice.
5. Cook the other waffles in a similar manner.

Nutritional value per serving: Calories: 164.6, Fat: 4.3 g, Carbohydrates: 28 g, Protein: 7.6 g

Ricotta and Yogurt Parfait

Level: Easy
Serves: 2
Preparation time: 5 minutes

Carbs: Moderate

Cooking time: 0 minutes

Ingredients:

- *1 ½ cups nonfat vanilla Greek yogurt*
- *1 teaspoon grated lemon zest*
- *2 tablespoons slivered almonds*
- *½ cup part-skim ricotta cheese*
- *½ cup raspberries*
- *2 teaspoons chia seeds*

Directions:

1. Mix the ricotta, yogurt, and lemon zest into a bowl.
2. Divide the mixture into two parfait glasses. Place ¼ cup raspberries, a tablespoon of almonds, and a teaspoon of the chia seeds in each glass and serve.

Nutritional value per serving: Calories: 173, Fat: 5.6 g, Carbohydrates: 19.7 g, Sugar: 13.4g, Protein: 11 g

Healthy Muffins

Level: Easy
Serves: 6
Preparation time: 10 minutes

Carbs: Moderate

Cooking time: 15 minutes

Ingredients:

- *¾ cup white whole-wheat flour*
- *½ teaspoon baking soda*
- *¼ cup coconut sugar or light brown sugar*
- *pinch of salt*
- *¼ cup maple syrup*
- *1 ½ tablespoons melted coconut oil*
- *1 large egg*
- *¼ cup unsweetened almond milk*
- *½ cup applesauce, unsweetened*

Directions:

1. Start by preheating your oven to 350 °F. Take a 6-count muffin pan and grease it with some cooking spray. Placing disposable liners in the cups is of great help. If you place the liners, spray the liners with cooking spray as well.
2. Sift the baking soda, flour, and salt into a bowl. Add sugar and stir.
3. Beat the egg in a bowl adding the maple syrup, milk, and applesauce.
4. Add the flour mixture to the egg mixture and stir well.
5. Stir in the coconut oil. Divide the batter into the muffin cups.

6. Place the muffin pan in the oven and bake for 18-22 minutes or until the muffins are cooked. Do a toothpick test by poking a toothpick in the center of a muffin. If you find any batter stuck on it after you take it out, you must bake it for a few more minutes.
7. Let the muffins cool in the pan on your countertop for about 5-8 minutes.
8. Take them out from the pan and serve warm.

Nutritional value per serving: Calories: 167, Fat: 5.1 g, Carbohydrates: 27.8 g, Sugar: 17.8 g, Protein: 3.3 g

Healthy Breakfast Rice

Level: Easy
Serves: 3
Preparation time: 10 minutes

Carbs: Moderate

Cooking time: 10 minutes

Ingredients:

- *¼ cup chopped green onion*
- *¼ cup diced onion*
- *½ tablespoon minced garlic*
- *½ cup frozen peas and carrots*
- *2 eggs, beaten*
- *4 slices turkey bacon, cooked, chopped into bite-size pieces*
- *1 ½ tablespoons coconut sugar (optional)*
- *2 tablespoons soy sauce or tamari*
- *⅛ teaspoon dry mustard*
- *1 cup diced bell pepper*
- *⅓ cup diced ham*
- *⅓ cup diced chicken sausage link*
- *1 ¼ cups a day old cooked brown rice, chilled*
- *½ tablespoon coconut oil*
- *salt and pepper to taste*

Directions:

1. Combine the soy sauce, mustard, and coconut sugar in a bowl.
2. Spray a pan with cooking spray. Add the beaten egg and stir often until the eggs are soft-cooked.
3. Add the coconut oil to a pan or wok and place it over medium-high heat. When the oil melts, add the garlic, onion, sausage, bell pepper, and ham and mix well.
4. Stir from time to time and cook for a couple of minutes.
5. Stir in the frozen peas and carrots, bacon, and rice. Add salt and pepper to taste.
6. Add the soy sauce mixture and mix well. Add the eggs and mix well. Heat thoroughly.
7. Turn off the heat. Add green onion and mix well.
8. Serve hot.

Nutritional value per serving: Calories: 284, Fat: 11 g, Carbohydrates: 33.1 g, Sugar: 2.3 g, Protein: 3.4 g

Brownie Batter Oatmeal

Level: Easy
Carbs: High
Serves: 1
Preparation time: 20 minutes
Cooking time: 5-6 minutes

Ingredients:
- *¼ cup pitted, chopped dates*
- *¼ cup ground almonds*
- *1 tablespoon cocoa*
- *½ teaspoon vanilla extract*
- *½ cup 2% milk*
- *3 tablespoons old-fashioned oats*
- *½ teaspoon butter*

To serve:
- *fresh raspberries*
- *almond slices*

Directions:
1. Place the dates in a bowl. Fill the bowl with boiling water. Soak the dates in the water for 10 minutes.
2. Retain 3-4 tablespoons of the soaked water and discard the rest.
3. Blend the dates and the retained water in a blender until you get a fine puree.
4. Combine the pureed dates, milk, oats, almonds, and cocoa in a saucepan.
5. Place the saucepan over medium heat. Stir occasionally until it comes to a boil.
6. Now turn off the heat. Add in the vanilla extract and butter. Stir until the butter melts and is well blended with the oatmeal.
7. Pour it into a bowl. Top with a couple of raspberries and sliced almonds, and serve.

Nutritional value per serving: Calories: 338, Fat: 17.8 g, Carbohydrates: 37 g, Protein: 12 g

Pumpkin Pie Oatmeal

Level: Easy
Carbs: High
Serves: 2
Preparation time: 3 minutes
Cooking time: 3 minutes

Ingredients:
- *1 cup rolled oats*
- *½ cup water*
- *½ teaspoon ground nutmeg*
- *1 teaspoon ground cinnamon*

- *2 tablespoons peanut butter*
- *1 cup of milk of your choice*
- *2 scoops vanilla protein powder*
- *1 cup pumpkin puree*

Directions:

1. Add the oatmeal, water, and milk into a saucepan and place it over medium heat.
2. Stir often and turn off the heat when it boils.
3. Stir in the spices, peanut butter, protein powder, and pumpkin puree.
4. Divide equally into two bowls and serve.

Nutritional value per serving: Calories: 447, Fat: 13.4 g, Carbs: 43 g, Sugar: 11 g, Protein: 36.7 g

Healthy Pancakes

Level: Easy
Serves: 2
Preparation time: 5 minutes
Carbs: High
Cooking time: 8 minutes

Ingredients:

- *1 egg*
- *⅓ cup almond milk or any non-dairy milk*
- *¾ teaspoon vanilla extract*
- *1 teaspoon baking powder*
- *1 cup low-fat plain or vanilla Greek yogurt*
- *1 tablespoon pure maple syrup*
- *1 cup rolled oats*
- *¼ teaspoon ground cinnamon*

For the toppings: Optional

- *chocolate chips*
- *blueberries*
- *chopped fresh fruit of your choice*
- *chia seeds*

For serving: Optional

- *maple syrup or honey*
- *butter*
- *fruits of your choice*
- *peanut butter*

Directions:

1. Blend the egg, milk, vanilla, baking powder, yogurt, maple syrup, oats, and cinnamon until well combined and free from lumps.
2. Pour the batter into a bowl and allow the batter to rest for about 10 minutes.
3. Heat a pan over medium and spray it with cooking spray.
4. Pour half of the batter into the pan. Sprinkle toppings over the batter if using.
5. When the underside of the pancake is golden brown, turn the pancake over and cook the other side.
6. Remove onto a plate and serve with any of the suggested serving options.
7. Similarly, make the other pancake (steps 3-6).

Nutritional value per serving: Calories: 239, Fat: 5.9 g, Carbs: 34 g, Sugar: 7.8 g, Protein: 10.1 g

Vegan Dark Chocolate Quinoa Bowl

Level: Easy
Serves: 2
Preparation time: 5 minutes

Carbs: High
Cooking time: 25 minutes

Ingredients:

For the quinoa bowl:

- *½ cup uncooked white quinoa, rinsed well*
- *½ cup light coconut milk*
- *1 tablespoon unsweetened cocoa powder*
- *¼ teaspoon vanilla extract*
- *½ cup unsweetened almond milk plus extra to serve*
- *wee bit of salt*
- *1 ½ tablespoons maple syrup or coconut sugar*
- *2 squares of vegan dark chocolate*

For the toppings: Optional

- *banana slices*
- *berries of your choice*
- *seeds of your choice*
- *vegan chocolate shavings*
- *any other toppings of your choice*

Directions:

1. Place a saucepan over medium heat. Wait for the pan to heat. Drain the quinoa and add to the saucepan.
2. Stir often until you get a nice, toasted aroma. Do not brown the quinoa; you should just lightly toast it.
3. Pour in the coconut milk and almond milk and stir. Add salt and stir. Once the mixture begins to boil, turn the heat to low and simmer until no milk is left in the saucepan and the quinoa is tender.
4. Turn off the heat. Stir in vanilla, maple syrup, and cocoa powder.
5. Divide the quinoa into two bowls. Top with a square of chocolate in each bowl. You can chop the chocolate if desired.
6. Serve topped with any of the suggested serving options if desired.

Nutritional value per serving: Calories: 236, Fat: 6.7 g, Carbs: 40.9 g, Sugar: 9 g, Protein: 7.5 g

Blueberry Baked Oatmeal

Level: Easy
Serves: 1
Preparation time: 5 minutes

Carbs: High

Cooking time: 10 minutes

Ingredients:

- *½ cup old-fashioned rolled oats*
- *¼ teaspoon aluminum-free baking powder*
- *⅛ teaspoon fine-grain sea salt*
- *¾ teaspoon ground flaxseeds*
- *½ teaspoon vanilla extract*
- *¼ cup + ⅛ cup fresh or frozen blueberries. divided*
- *1 tablespoon pure maple syrup*
- *½ teaspoon ground cinnamon*
- *½ cup unsweetened vanilla-flavored almond milk*
- *½ tablespoon coconut oil melted*
- *½ ripe banana, mashed*
- *cooking spray*

To serve: Optional

- *blueberries*
- *maple syrup*
- *peanut butter or almond butter*

Directions:

1. Start by preheating your oven to 375 °F. Take a ramekin or a small baking dish (about 4 inches) and grease it with cooking spray.
2. You now have to make the oatmeal mixture, so add the oats, cinnamon, baking powder, and salt into a bowl and mix it up.
3. Next, add the milk, ground flaxseed, vanilla, maple syrup, coconut oil, and mashed banana into the bowl and stir until well incorporated. If you do not have ground flaxseed, you can beat a small egg and use half of it.
4. Scatter ¼ cup blueberries over the batter and fold the berries into the batter.
5. Spoon the mixture in the baking dish and spread evenly.
6. Top with the remaining ⅛ cup blueberries and put the baking dish into the oven for about 30 minutes or until golden brown.
7. Once it is done with the baking, take out the baking dish and allow it to cool for about 10 minutes.
8. Serve topped with blueberries, maple syrup, and peanut butter if desired.

Nutritional value per serving: Calories: 395.6, Fat: 14.4 g, Carbs: 65.4 g, Sugar: 27.6 g, Protein: 8.3 g

Oatmeal with Tofu (Vegan)

Level: Easy
Carbs: High
Serves: 2
Preparation time: 5 minutes
Cooking time: 12-15 minutes

Ingredients:

- *½ cup old-fashioned rolled oats*
- *¼ teaspoon salt*
- *6 ounces of silken tofu*
- *2 very ripe bananas*
- *1 ½ cups water*
- *½ teaspoon cinnamon*
- *1 teaspoon vanilla extract*

To serve: Optional

- *peanut butter or almond butter*
- *yogurt*
- *fresh fruit of your choice*
- *chocolate chips*
- *any other toppings of your choice*

Directions:

1. Add the oats, cinnamon, salt, and water into a pot and place the pot over medium-high heat.
2. When the mixture starts boiling, turn the heat to medium and cook until nearly dry. Make sure to stir often to avoid burning the oats.
3. Meanwhile, place the tofu in a blender and blend until smooth.
4. Add the blended tofu into the pot and keep stirring until heated thoroughly.
5. Next, you need to add the banana and vanilla and give it a good stir.
6. Take the pan off the heat. Let it rest covered for about 5 minutes.
7. Stir and serve.

Nutritional value per serving: Calories: 236, Fat: 4.3 g, Carbohydrates: 43.4 g, Sugar: 15.3 g, Protein: 7.8 g

Baked French Toast Casserole

Level: Easy
Carbs: High
Serves: 4
Preparation time: 5 minutes plus chilling time
Cooking time: 30 minutes

Ingredients:

- *½ loaf whole-wheat bread cut into 1-inch cubes*
- *1 ⅛ cups milk*
- *¼ teaspoon ground cinnamon*
- *⅛ teaspoon salt*
- *3 eggs*
- *½ tablespoon pure maple syrup or light brown sugar*
- *1 teaspoon vanilla extract*

For the topping:

- *1 tablespoon pure maple syrup or light brown sugar*
- *2 tablespoons unsalted butter, melted*
- *¼ teaspoon ground cinnamon*

To serve: Optional

- *maple syrup or honey*
- *fresh fruit of your choice*

Directions:

1. Coat a 6-7 inch baking dish with cooking spray.
2. Scatter the bread cubes evenly in the dish.
3. Beat the eggs in a bowl adding the milk, cinnamon, salt, vanilla, and maple syrup.
4. Drizzle this mixture all over the bread cubes. Next, add the maple syrup, butter, and cinnamon into a bowl and whisk well. Trickle this mixture all over the bread cubes.
5. Cover the dish with foil and chill for 1-8 hours, depending on your time.
6. The next thing is to preheat your oven to 350 °F.
7. Bake the casserole for 20 minutes. Uncover and bake for 10 more minutes or until it turns light brown.
8. Serve with the suggested serving options if desired.

Nutritional value per serving: Calories: 316.7, Fat: 13 g, Carbohydrates: 39 g, Sugar: 8.9 g, Protein: 13.1 g

Vegan Omelet

Level: Easy
Serves: 2
Preparation time: 10 minutes

Carbs: High

Cooking time: 20 minutes

Ingredients:

- *1 ⅓ cups chickpea flour*
- *¼ teaspoon pepper or to taste*
- *½ teaspoon garlic powder*
- *½ teaspoon salt or to taste*
- *1 teaspoon turmeric powder*
- *1 teaspoon baking powder*
- *2 teaspoons apple cider vinegar*
- *¼ teaspoon Himalayan pink salt (optional)*
- *2 tablespoons nutritional yeast*
- *1 ½ cups water*

For the filling:

- *4 cloves garlic, peeled, minced*
- *½ cup chopped red bell pepper*
- *1 green onion, thinly sliced*
- *4 mushrooms, chopped*
- *4 small tomatoes, chopped*

Directions:

1. Combine the chickpea flour, spices, and baking powder in a mixing bowl.
2. Pour in the water and vinegar and whisk with a hand whisk until smooth and free from lumps.
3. Stir in the nutritional yeast. You should have a batter of the consistency of a pancake. So, add more water if the batter is thick. It should be a pourable batter.
4. Place a non-stick pan over medium heat. Spray some cooking spray into the pan.
5. Cook the garlic and mushrooms in the pan for a couple of minutes. Stir in the bell pepper and cook until tender.
6. Stir in the green onion and tomatoes. Remove the vegetables onto a plate after about a minute.
7. Clean the pan and spray the pan with some cooking oil spray. Pour half of the batter into the pan and spread gently. Cover the pan and cook until the underside is golden brown.
8. Turn the omelet over and cook uncovered for about 2-3 minutes. Scatter half the vegetables all over the omelet. Now cook covered until the omelet is cooked through. Transfer onto a plate and serve.
9. Similarly, make the other omelet (steps 8 and 9).

Nutritional value per serving: Calories: 371, Fat: 4.6 g, Carbohydrates: 51 g, Sugar: 13.8 g, Protein: 19 g

Breakfast Bake

Level: Easy
Serves: 3
Preparation time: 15 minutes

Carbs: High

Cooking time: 40 minutes

Ingredients:

- *1 ½ tablespoons olive oil, divided*
- *½ onion, thinly sliced*
- *3 cups chopped fresh spinach leaves*
- *red pepper flakes to taste*
- *freshly ground black pepper to taste*
- *2 egg whites*
- *2 eggs*
- *¾ teaspoon whole-grain mustard*
- *1 ½ tablespoons finely chopped fresh chives*
- *2 cups whole-wheat bread, cut into 1-inch cubes*
- *1 clove garlic, finely chopped*
- *¼ teaspoon grated lemon zest*
- *salt to taste*
- *¾ cup whole milk*
- *3 tablespoons grated parmesan cheese divided*

Directions:

1. Grease a baking dish (about 7-8 inches) with ½ tablespoon of oil.
2. Spread the bread cubes in the baking dish.
3. Heat a tablespoon of oil in a pan over medium heat.
4. Drop the garlic and onion into the hot oil and stir. Cook until the onion is slightly caramelized.
5. Stir in the spinach. Cook until the spinach turns limp.
6. Add the seasonings and stir, then add the lemon zest. Keep stirring for a few more seconds, careful not to burn the seasonings. Take it off the heat and allow it to cool for a few minutes.
7. Next is preheating your oven to 350 °F.
8. Add the egg whites, eggs, mustard, and milk into a bowl and whisk well.
9. Stir in 2 tablespoons of the parmesan, salt, and pepper.
10. Add in the spinach mixture and chives and give it a good stir.
11. Spoon the mixture over the bread cubes in the baking dish. Sprinkle a tablespoon of parmesan cheese on top and place it in the oven.
12. Bake until the egg mixture is set. Cool for 10 minutes and serve.

Nutritional value per serving: Calories: 466.4, Fat: 19.7 g, Carbohydrates: 44.6 g, Sugar: 8.4 g, Protein: 23.8 g

Chickpea and Sweet Potato Breakfast Hash

Level: Easy
Serves: 6
Preparation time: 10 minutes
Carbs: High
Cooking time: 35-40 minutes

Ingredients:

- *3 pounds sweet potatoes, peeled, cut into about 1-inch cubes*
- *1 green bell pepper, deseeded, diced*
- *2 red bell peppers, deseeded, diced*
- *1 yellow bell pepper, deseeded, diced*
- *2 cans (15 ounces each) of chickpeas, drained, rinsed*
- *2 teaspoons garlic powder*
- *freshly cracked pepper to taste*

For the spicy tahini sauce:

- *½ cup water*
- *½ cup tahini*
- *juice of a lemon or to taste*
- *sriracha sauce as per your taste*
- *salt to taste*

Directions:

1. Start by preheating your oven to 425 °F. On a large baking sheet, place a sheet of parchment paper. Mix the sweet potatoes, bell peppers, onions, and chickpeas in a large bowl.
2. Add oil, salt, pepper, and garlic powder and mix well.
3. Spread the mixture on the baking sheet without overlay.
4. Bake for 20 minutes. Stir the mixture after baking for about 10 minutes.
5. Increase the oven's heat to 500 °F, stir the mixture again, and bake for 20 minutes.
6. To make the dressing: Add the water, salt, tahini, lemon juice, and sriracha sauce into a bowl and mix well. Cover the bowl and keep it aside for the flavors to meld.
7. Serve the hash in bowls. Drizzle sauce on top and serve with toppings of your choice.

Nutritional value per serving: Calories: 391, Fat: 7.1 g, Carbohydrates: 73 g, Sugar: 17.4 g, Protein: 10.8 g

Cherry and Almond Oatmeal

Level: Easy
Serves: 3
Preparation time: 5 minutes
Carbs: High
Cooking time: 10 minutes

Ingredients:

- *2 cups vanilla almond milk*
- *½ cup dried cherries*
- *¼ teaspoon salt*
- *½ cup steel-cut oats*
- *3 tablespoons packed brown sugar*
- *¼ teaspoon ground cinnamon*

Directions:

1. Combine the milk, cherries, salt, oats, brown sugar, and cinnamon in a saucepan.
2. Over low heat, cook the mixture stirring often.

Nutritional value per serving: Calories: 277, Fat: 3.4 g, Carbohydrates: 56.7 g, Sugar: 34.5 g, Protein: 4.9 g

Bean and Avocado Toast

Level: Super easy
Serves: 2
Preparation time: 5 minutes
Carbs: High
Cooking time: 2-3 minutes

Ingredients:

- *2 slices whole-wheat bread*
- *1 cup canned white beans, drained*
- *Pepper to taste*
- *½ avocado, mashed*
- *Salt to taste*
- *Crushed red pepper to taste*

Directions:

1. Toast the bread slices to the desired crispiness.
2. Spread the avocado over the toast. Top with beans. Sprinkle salt, crushed red pepper, and pepper.

Nutritional value per serving: Calories: 230.7, Fat: 8.9 g, Carbohydrates: 33.8 g, Sugar: 3.2 g, Protein: 11.2 g

Berry Chia Pudding

Level: Easy
Serves: 4

Carbs: High
Preparation time: 10 minutes

Ingredients:

- *3 ½ cups blackberries or raspberries, fresh or frozen*
- *½ cup chia seeds*
- *1 ½ teaspoons vanilla extract*
- *½ cup granola*
- *2 cups unsweetened almond milk or any milk of your preference*
- *2 tablespoons pure maple syrup*
- *1 cup full-fat plain Greek yogurt*

Directions:

1. The night before: Add 2 ½ cups of berries into a blender and blend until smooth.
2. Pour the blended berries into a bowl. Add maple syrup, chia seeds, and vanilla and mix well.
3. Keep the bowl covered in the refrigerator all night.
4. The following morning, assemble the pudding. Take four glasses or bowls and layer with the pudding, remaining berries, and yogurt in whatever manner you desire. Top with granola and serve.

Nutritional value per serving: Calories: 343, Fat: 14.5 g, Carbohydrates: 38.9 g, Sugar: 17.8 g, Protein: 14.4 g

Chapter 6: Lunch Recipes

LOW-CARB RECIPES

Chicken and White Bean Soup

Level: Easy

Carbs: Low

Serves: 3

Preparation time: 5-8 minutes

Cooking time: 15 minutes

Ingredients:

- *1 teaspoon extra-virgin olive oil*
- *½ tablespoon chopped fresh sage or ¼ teaspoon dried sage*
- *1 cup water*
- *2 cups boneless, skinless, shredded roasted chicken*
- *1 leek, white and light green part, cut into ¼ inch wide, round slices*
- *2 cups chicken broth*
- *¾ cup canned cannellini beans, rinsed, drained*
- *salt to taste (optional)*
- *pepper to taste*

Directions:

1. Pour the oil into a Dutch oven or soup pot and let it heat over medium-high heat. Once the oil is hot, add leeks and cook until tender.
2. Add the sage and cook for a few seconds, stirring constantly until you get a nice aroma.
3. Add the broth and water, and turn up the heat to high. Cover the pot. When the soup starts boiling, stir in the chicken and beans. Heat thoroughly and serve.

Nutritional value per serving: Calories: 248, Fat: 5.8 g, Carbohydrates: 14.8 g, Sugar: 1 g, Protein: 35.1 g

Vegetable Soup

Level: Easy
Serves: 6
Preparation time: 10 minutes
Carbs: Low
Cooking time: 20 minutes

Ingredients:

- *1 tablespoon olive oil*
- *1 large bell pepper, diced*
- *½ medium head cauliflower, cut into 1-inch florets*
- *1 can (14.5 ounces) diced tomatoes*
- *½ large onion, diced*
- *2 cloves garlic, peeled, minced*
- *1 cup green beans pieces (1-inch pieces)*
- *4 cups vegetable or chicken broth*
- *1 bay leaf*
- *pepper to taste*
- *½ tablespoon Italian seasoning*
- *salt to taste*

Directions:

1. Heat a soup pot over medium heat, and add oil to it
2. Add the bell pepper and onion into the hot oil and stir. Cook until the onion is light brown.
3. Add the garlic. Stir until it gets aromatic.
4. Next, the cauliflower and beans, broth, tomatoes, bay leaves, and seasonings will be added to the pot.
5. When the soup starts boiling, boil the heat to medium-low and simmer until the vegetables are tender.
6. Ladle into soup bowls and serve.

Nutritional value per serving: Calories: 62, Fat: 2.9 g, Carbohydrates: 7.8 g, Sugar: 3.9 g, Protein: 2.8 g

Chicken Soup with Vegetables

Level: Easy
Carbs: Low
Serves: 3
Preparation time: 10 minutes
Cooking time: 25 minutes

Ingredients:

- *1 tablespoon extra-virgin olive oil*
- *4 ounces sliced cremini mushrooms*
- *1 carrot, thinly sliced*
- *½ medium onion, chopped*
- *1 stalk celery, thinly sliced*
- *1 tablespoon minced garlic*
- *⅛ teaspoon cayenne pepper or to taste*
- *1 pound bone-in chicken thighs, skinless*
- *¼ teaspoon salt or to taste*
- *1 cup chopped lacinato kale leaves (no stems)*
- *1 teaspoon chopped fresh sage*
- *2 small bay leaves*
- *4 cups chicken broth*
- *¼ teaspoon pepper or to taste*
- *1 tablespoon fresh lemon juice*

Directions:

1. Heat a soup pot over medium-high heat and pour some oil in it.
2. Add the carrot, celery, mushrooms, and onion into the hot oil and stir.
3. Stir on and off until the veggies are slightly brown.
4. Add the garlic, bay leaves, cayenne pepper, and sage, and keep stirring for a few seconds until you get a nice aroma.
5. Add the broth, chicken, pepper, and salt.
6. When the soup starts boiling, cook until the chicken is tender.
7. Remove the chicken from the pot and place on a plate.
8. Add the kale to the soup and cook until kale wilts. Turn off the heat.
9. Meanwhile, shred the chicken with a pair of forks and add only the meat to the soup.
10. Stir well and serve.

Nutritional value per serving: Calories: 261, Fat: 11.2 g, Carbohydrates: 10.1 g, Sugar: 4.3 g, Protein: 26.7 g

Grilled Chicken

Level: Easy
Serves: 2
Preparation time: 15 minutes plus chilling time

Carbs: Low
Cooking time: 10 minutes

Ingredients:

- *14 ounces of boneless, skinless chicken breasts*
- *2 large cloves garlic, peeled, minced*
- *¼ teaspoon dried oregano*
- *½ teaspoon dried thyme*
- *Salt to taste*
- *¾ teaspoon grated lemon zest*
- *3 tablespoons extra-virgin olive oil + extra for greasing the grill grate*
- *Freshly ground black pepper to taste*

Directions:

1. Place the chicken over a sheet of plastic wrap on your countertop. Cover the chicken with another sheet of plastic wrap and beat with a meat tenderizer until it is ½ inch thick.
2. Combine the garlic, oregano, thyme, salt, lemon zest, and oil in a Ziploc bag.
3. Place the chicken in the bag. Seal the bag and turn the bag around a few times until the chicken is well coated with the marinade. Refrigerate for 1-4 hours
4. Set your grill to high heat and preheat the grill. Grease the grill grates with some oil.
5. Lay the chicken on the grill grate and cover the grill. Cook for 2-3 minutes. Turn the chicken over and cook the other side for 2-3 minutes. Do not grill for longer than 3 minutes on each side.
6. Serve hot. You can serve it as it is or with steamed or grilled vegetables.

Nutritional value per serving: ½ recipe, Calories: 413, Fat: 24 g, Carbohydrates: 1.9 g, Sugar: 0 g, Protein: 41.2 g

Cajun Shrimp and Sausage Vegetable Skillet

Level: Easy
Serves: 3
Preparation time: 5 minutes

Carbs: Low
Cooking time: 10 minutes

Ingredients:

- *7 ounces of chicken sausage, sliced*
- *½ pound large shrimp, peeled, deveined*
- *1 medium zucchini, trimmed, sliced*
- *¼ bunch of asparagus, cut into thirds*
- *1 medium yellow squash, sliced*
- *1 red bell pepper, cut into 1-inch squares*
- *1 tablespoon olive oil*
- *salt to taste*
- *pepper to taste*
- *1 tablespoon Cajun seasoning*

Directions:

1. Place the sausage, shrimp, squash, bell pepper, zucchini, and asparagus in a bowl and toss well.
2. Drizzle oil over the mixture. Season with pepper, salt, and Cajun seasoning. Toss well.
3. Place a skillet over medium-high heat. When the skillet is hot, add the shrimp mixture. Keep stirring until the shrimp becomes pink. It should take you around 5-6 minutes.
4. Sprinkle parsley on top and serve.

Nutritional value per serving: Calories: 262.3, Fat: 12.4 g, Carbohydrates: 7.8 g, Sugar: 4.5 g, Protein: 29.8 g

Cod and Asparagus Bake

Level: Easy
Carbs: Low
Serves: 2
Preparation time: 10 minutes
Cooking time: 5 minutes

Ingredients:

- *2 cod filets (4 ounces each)*
- *1 cup cherry tomatoes, halved*
- *¾ teaspoon grated lemon zest*
- *½ pound fresh, thin asparagus, trimmed*
- *1 tablespoon of lemon juice*
- *⅛ cup grated Romano cheese*

Directions:

1. Start by preheating your oven to 375 °F. Grease a baking dish with oil.
2. Put the cod and asparagus in the baking dish. Add the tomatoes to the baking dish skin side up.
3. Brush lemon juice on top of the fish. Scatter lemon zest on top. Scatter cheese all over.
4. Place it in the oven and set the timer for 12 minutes or bake until the fish is cooked and can be pierced readily with a fork. Take out the baking dish.
5. Turn the oven to broil mode and let it preheat.
6. Place the baking sheet in the oven about 3-4 inches below the heating element.
7. Broil for 3-4 minutes.
8. Serve hot.

Nutritional value per serving: Calories: 141, Fat: 3.3 g, Carbohydrates: 5.6 g, Sugar: 3.1 g, Protein: 22.3 g

Chipotle-Orange Broccoli and Tofu

Level: Easy
Serves: 2
Preparation time: 10 minutes
Carbs: Low
Cooking time: 20 minutes

Ingredients:

- *7 ounces extra-firm, water-packed tofu, drained, cut into cubes*
- *1 ½ tablespoons canola oil, divided*
- *½ cup fresh orange juice*
- *¼ cup chopped fresh cilantro*
- *Salt to taste*
- *3 cups broccoli florets*
- *½ tablespoon minced chipotle chili in adobo sauce*

Directions:

1. Add a tablespoon of oil to a non-stick pan and place it over medium-high heat.
2. Season the tofu with salt and place in the pan without overlapping.
3. Cook until they turn golden brown all over. Stir occasionally.
4. Remove the tofu from the pan and place on a plate.
5. Heat the remaining oil in the same pan. Add the broccoli and season with salt. Stir on and off for a couple of minutes until they turn brilliant green.
6. Stir in the orange juice and chipotle chili. Stir on and off for about a minute.
7. Add the tofu back into the pan. Mix well. Add cilantro and stir. Serve hot.

Nutritional value per serving: Calories: 241, Fat: 16.7 g, Carbohydrates: 14.3 g, Sugar: 5.6 g, Protein: 13.9 g

Apple and Spinach Salad with Honey Balsamic Vinaigrette

Level: Easy
Serves: 2
Preparation time: 10 minutes
Carbs: Low
Cooking time: 10 minutes

Ingredients:

- *3 cups fresh spinach leaves*
- *⅓ cup feta cheese*
- *¼ cup chopped walnuts*
- *¼ cup dried cranberries*
- *¼ small red onion, sliced*
- *½ large apple, cored, chopped*

For the honey balsamic vinaigrette:

- *⅓ cup olive oil*
- *1 teaspoon minced garlic*
- *½ teaspoon Dijon mustard*
- *⅛ teaspoon ground black pepper*

- *3 tablespoons balsamic vinegar*
- *½ tablespoon honey*
- *pinch of sea salt*
- *⅛ teaspoon dried basil*

Directions:

1. After you rinse the spinach leaves, dry them properly, or your salad will be soggy. You can dry the leaves by patting them with a paper towel.
2. Combine the spinach, feta cheese, walnuts, cranberries, onion, and apple in a bowl.
3. To make the dressing: Add the olive oil, garlic, Dijon mustard, black pepper, balsamic vinegar, honey, salt, and basil into a small jar. Fasten the lid and shake vigorously for a few seconds until well combined.
4. Use as much dressing as required and store the remaining in the refrigerator. It can last for 5-6 days.
5. Pour the dressing over the salad. Toss well and serve.

Nutritional value per serving: Calories: 177, Fat: 12.8 g, Carbs: 14.1 g, Sugar: 8.1 g, Protein: 6.7 g

For the honey balsamic vinaigrette:

Nutritional value per serving: Calories: 156, Fat: 16.7 g, Carbs: 2.6 g, Sugar: 2.2 g, Protein: 0.1 g

---

Chicken Cobb Salad

Level: Easy
Serves: 2
Carbs: Low
Preparation time: 10 minutes

Ingredients:

For the dressing:

- *4 tablespoons blue cheese dressing*
- *1 teaspoon pepper or to taste*
- *¼ teaspoon salt*

For the filling:

- *1 small tomato, chopped*
- *1 tablespoon bacon bits*
- *1 cup chopped romaine lettuce*
- *1 cup shredded rotisserie chicken*
- *2 hard-boiled eggs, peeled, chopped*

Directions:

1. Mix the salt, pepper, and blue cheese dressing in a bowl.
2. Stir in the chicken, tomato, eggs, bacon bits, and lettuce.
3. You can serve it chilled or at room temperature.

Nutritional value per serving: Calories: 407, Fat: 27.1g, Carbs: 5.6g, Sugar: 2.3 g, Protein: 31.2 g

Ranch Chicken Salad

Level: Easy
Serves: 2
Preparation time: 20 minutes
Carbs: Low
Cooking time: 7 minutes

Ingredients:

- *½ tablespoon olive oil*
- *Salt to taste*
- *Pepper to taste*
- *2 cups romaine lettuce, torn into bite-size pieces*
- *½ cup round cucumber slices*
- *½ cup shredded mozzarella cheese*
- *½ boneless, skinless chicken breast cut into bite-size pieces*
- *¼ cup ranch dressing*
- *½ cup cherry tomatoes*
- *½ bell pepper, diced*

To serve:

- *½ cup whole-wheat tortilla strips*

Directions:

1. Pour the olive oil into a non-stick pan and let it heat over medium heat. Season the chicken with salt and pepper and place in the pan.
2. Cook until the chicken is well-cooked inside. Take it off the heat and cool it down.
3. Combine the chicken, bell peppers, cheese, cucumber, lettuce, and tomatoes in a bowl.
4. Add the ranch dressing and mix well.
5. Add the tortilla strips. Mix well and serve.

Nutritional value per serving: Calories: 417.1, Fat: 27.8g, Carbs: 7.8g, Sugar: 4.3g, Protein: 32.1g

Minty Watermelon Cucumber Salad

Level: Easy
Serves: 4
Carbs: Low
Preparation time: 10 minutes

Ingredients:

- *2 cups seedless watermelon cubes*
- *1 ½ green onions, chopped*
- *1 tablespoon balsamic vinegar*
- *⅛ teaspoon salt*
- *½ English cucumber, halved lengthwise, sliced crosswise*
- *1 tablespoon minced fresh mint*
- *1 tablespoon olive oil*
- *⅛ teaspoon pepper*

Directions:

1. Whisk together the vinegar, oil, salt, pepper, and mint in a bowl.
2. Add the cucumber and watermelon and mix well.

Nutritional value per serving: Calories: 61.8, Fat: 3.2 g, Carbs: 8.9 g, Sugar: 7.8 g, Protein: 0.8 g

Buffalo Chicken Salad

Level: Easy
Serves: 4
Preparation time: 10 minutes

Carbs: Low

Cooking time: 15 minutes

Ingredients:

- *½ cup cooked, shredded chicken*
- *1 teaspoon chopped fresh parsley*
- *⅛ teaspoon garlic powder*
- *⅛ cup blue cheese crumbles (optional)*
- *6 tablespoons nonfat plain Greek yogurt*
- *¼ cup finely diced celery*
- *1 tablespoon buffalo sauce*

Directions:

1. You can cook the chicken in a pot of boiling water, a crockpot, or an instant pot. You can also use rotisserie chicken.
2. Combine the chicken, parsley, yogurt, cheese, buffalo sauce, and garlic powder in a bowl.
3. You can serve as it is or over a bed of lettuce leaves. You can also serve it as a filling for sandwiches. Of course, the nutritional value will change.

Nutritional value per serving: Calories: 257.8, Fat: 4.5 g, Carbohydrates: 3.2 g, Sugar: 1.9 g, Protein: 46.7 g

MODERATE-CARB RECIPES

Asian Lettuce Wraps

Level: Easy
Serves: 2
Preparation time: 10 minutes

Carbs: Moderate

Cooking time: 10 minutes

Ingredients:

- *4 ½ teaspoons olive oil, divided*
- *2-3 tablespoons hoisin sauce or to taste*
- *1 teaspoon sriracha sauce (optional)*
- *¾ teaspoon sesame oil*
- *½ tablespoon peeled, minced fresh ginger*
- *¼ cup shredded carrot*
- *½ large head of Bibb lettuce or iceberg lettuce, separate the leaves*
- *½ pound 93% lean ground turkey or chicken*
- *½ tablespoon soy sauce*
- *½ tablespoon rice vinegar*
- *½ tablespoon minced garlic*
- *⅓ cup sliced green onions (white and light green parts only)*

- *⅛ cup sliced green onion (dark green part only) to garnish*
- *½ can (from 8 ounces can) of water chestnuts, drained, chopped*

Directions:

1. Place a non-stick pan over medium-high heat. Add a teaspoon of oil and let it heat up.
2. Place the meat in the pan and cook until light brown. Stir the meat. As you stir, crumble the meat. Cook for about 3 minutes or until well cooked.
3. Mix the soy sauce, sriracha, hoisin sauce, sesame oil, and rice vinegar in a bowl.
4. Discard any extra cooked fat from the pan and move the turkey to one side of the pan.
5. Add the remaining oil to the center of the skillet. When the oil is hot, add the carrot and green onion (white and light green parts) and mix well. Cook for a couple of minutes.
6. Stir in the ginger and garlic. Keep stirring until you get a pleasant aroma.
7. Add the sauce mixture and stir. Stir in the water chestnuts and heat thoroughly.
8. Take it off the heat and allow it to cool for 5-8 minutes.
9. Place the lettuce leaves on a serving platter. Place the turkey mixture on the lettuce leaves. Sprinkle the dark green onion slices on top and serve.

Nutritional value per serving: Calories: 303, Fat: 13.8g, Carbs: 19.2g, Sugar: 7.8g, Protein: 23.5g

Shrimp Cauliflower Gnocchi

Level: Easy
Carbs: Moderate
Serves: 2
Preparation time: 5 minutes
Cooking time: 15 minutes

Ingredients:

- *6 ounces of frozen cauliflower gnocchi*
- *½ tablespoon olive oil*
- *large pinch-dried oregano*
- *½ pound cooked, peeled shrimp, thaw it if it is frozen*
- *1 cup grape tomatoes, halved*
- *1 teaspoon minced garlic*
- *salt to taste*

Directions:

1. Follow the instructions given on the package of cauliflower gnocchi and cook the gnocchi.
2. Place the tomatoes, garlic, oil, salt, and oregano in a microwave-safe bowl. Place it in the microwave and cook on high until the tomatoes are soft. You can cook it in a pan over medium-low heat on your stovetop.
3. Add the shrimp and cauliflower gnocchi and mix well.

Nutritional value per serving: Calories: 132.3, Fat: 5.6 g, Carbohydrates: 17.3 g, Sugar: 3.4 g, Protein: 1.8 g

Kale and Brussels Sprouts Salad

Level: Easy
Serves: 3

Carbs: Moderate
Preparation time: 10 minutes

Ingredients:

- *4 ounces kale, discard stems and hard ribs, thinly sliced (around 3 cups)*
- *¼ cup chopped pistachios*
- *⅛ cup shredded parmesan cheese*
- *¼ pound Brussels sprouts, thinly sliced*
- *¼ cup honey mustard salad dressing*

Directions:

1. Add the kale, pistachios, parmesan, and Brussels sprouts into a bowl and toss well.
2. Pour the dressing over the salad. Mix well and serve.

Nutritional value per serving: Calories: 207, Fat: 13.9 g, Carbohydrates: 17.2 g, Sugar: 4.7 g, Protein: 7.8 g

Turkey Sandwich

Level: Easy
Serves: 2

Carbs: Moderate
Preparation time: 5 minutes

Ingredients:

- *4 slices of whole-wheat bread*
- *8 ounces sliced or shaved deli turkey*
- *lettuce leaves*
- *salt to taste*
- *pepper to taste*
- *4 tablespoons mayonnaise*
- *8 slices provolone cheese*
- *4 fresh tomato slices*

Directions:

1. Lather a tablespoon of mayonnaise on each bread slice.
2. Place the turkey slices on two of the bread slices on the mayonnaise side. Place two cheese slices and two tomato slices over the turkey on each. Season with salt and pepper. Add lettuce leaves.
3. Cover the sandwich with the remaining two bread slices with the mayonnaise side facing down.
4. Cut the sandwich into the desired shape and serve.

Nutritional value per serving: Calories: 719, Fat: 43.4 g, Carbohydrates: 31.2 g, Sugar: 8.1 g, Protein: 44.5 g

White Bean and Veggie Salad

Level: Easy
Serves: 2
Carbs: Moderate
Preparation time: 8-10 minutes

Ingredients:

- *4 cups mixed salad greens*
- *2/3 cup canned white beans, drained, rinsed*
- *1 ½ cups mixed vegetables of your choice*
- *1 avocado, peeled, pitted, diced*
- *4 teaspoons extra-virgin olive oil*
- *Freshly ground pepper to taste*
- *2 tablespoons red wine vinegar*
- *½ teaspoon kosher salt*

Directions:

1. For the mixed vegetables, you can choose something like cucumber, cherry tomatoes, carrots, radishes, or any other vegetables you choose.
2. Add the chosen vegetables, avocado, mixed salad greens, white beans, salt, pepper, olive oil, and red wine vinegar into a bowl and toss well.
3. Divide the salad into two bowls and serve.

Nutritional value per serving: Calories: 359, Fat: 24.6 g, Carbohydrates: 29.7 g, Sugar: 3 g, Protein: 10.1 g

---

Quick Quesadillas

Level: Easy
Serves: 2
Preparation time: 5 minutes
Carbs: Moderate
Cooking time: 8-10 minutes

Ingredients:

- *2 whole-wheat tortillas (8 inches each)*
- *½ cup cooked or canned black beans or pinto beans, drained, rinsed*
- *⅛ cup chopped red or green onion*
- *2 teaspoons olive oil or melted butter to brush*
- *1 cup freshly grated cheddar cheese*
- *⅛ cup chopped red bell pepper or thinly sliced cherry tomatoes*
- *⅛ cup chopped pickled jalapeños (optional)*

To serve: Optional

- *salsa*
- *guacamole*
- *pico de gallo*
- *chopped cilantro*
- *hot sauce*
- *sour cream*

Directions:

1. Heat a skillet over medium heat and lay a tortilla in it. After heating for 15 seconds, turn the tortilla over and let it heat for another 15 seconds.
2. Scatter ¼ cup cheese on one half of the tortilla. Scatter half of each-black beans, onion, red bell pepper, and jalapeños if using. Add ¼ cup cheese over the filling.
3. Fold the tortilla over the filling. Press with a spatula. So now the quesadilla is in a semi-circular shape.
4. Brush ½ teaspoon of oil immediately on one side of the tortilla and flip sides.
5. Brush ½ teaspoon of oil on top of the tortilla. Cook until crisp and brown.
6. Turn the quesadilla over and cook the other side until golden brown.
7. Transfer the quesadilla onto your cutting board and set aside to cool for about 1 minute.
8. Meanwhile, similarly make the other quesadilla (steps 1-7)
9. Cut the quesadilla into wedges and serve with any suggested options.

Nutritional value per serving: Calories: 459, Fat: 27.5 g, Carbohydrates: 31.3 g, Sugar: 2.4 g, Protein: 7.9 g

Grilled Veggie Pizza

Level: Easy
Carbs: Moderate
Serves: 3
Preparation time: 10 minutes
Cooking time: 20 minutes

Ingredients:

- *4 small fresh button mushrooms, halved*
- *½ small red bell pepper sliced*
- *½ small yellow bell pepper sliced*
- *½ small zucchini, cut into ¼ inch thick, round slices*
- *½ small onion, sliced*
- *1 small tomato chopped*
- *½ tablespoon water*
- *1 teaspoon minced fresh basil or ¼ teaspoon dried basil*
- *⅛ teaspoon pepper*
- *½ cup pizza sauce*
- *1 cup shredded part-skim mozzarella cheese*
- *½ tablespoon white wine vinegar*
- *2 teaspoons olive oil, divided*
- *⅛ teaspoon salt or to taste*
- *1 (6-inch) prebaked, thin, whole-wheat pizza crust*

Directions:

1. Preheat the oven on broil mode to medium heat.
2. Add the mushrooms, bell peppers, zucchini, onion, water, 1 ½ teaspoons of oil, salt, and pepper into a bowl and mix well.
3. Heat a grill pan over medium. When the pan is hot, add the vegetable mixture and spread it all over it. Cover and cook for 4-5 minutes. Do not stir during this time.
4. Now give it a good stir. Cover and cook for 4 more minutes. Take it off the heat.

5. Brush ½ teaspoon of oil on top of the pizza crust. Spread pizza sauce on the crust.
6. Next, spread the grilled vegetables on the crust. Scatter tomatoes and cheese.
7. Place the pizza directly on the rack in the oven. Bake for 8 minutes or until the cheese melts, as per your preference.
8. Cut into three wedges and serve.

Nutritional value per serving: Calories: 273, Fat: 11.1 g, Carbohydrates: 29.4 g, Sugar: 5.8 g, Protein: 17.3 g

---

Farro Salad

Level: Easy
Carbs: Moderate
Serves: 2
Preparation time: 10 minutes
Cooking time: 20 minutes

Ingredients:

- *2 tablespoons lemon juice*
- *1 ½ cups cooked farro*
- *½ cup fresh mint leaves, torn*
- *2 whole, canned artichoke hearts, rinsed, chopped*
- *¼ cup chopped, salted, roasted pistachio nuts*
- *3 tablespoons pomegranate seeds or dried cranberries*
- *1 ½ ounces soft goat cheese, crumbled*
- *2 tablespoons extra-virgin olive oil*
- *3 cups packed baby arugula*
- *¼ cup thinly sliced fresh basil leaves*
- *¼ teaspoon salt or to taste*

Directions:

1. Combine the farro, herbs, salt, artichoke, and arugula in a bowl.
2. Drizzle lemon juice and oil over the salad. Toss well.
3. Garnish with pomegranate, pistachios, and goat cheese, and serve.

Nutritional value per serving: Calories: 503, Fat: 31 g, Carbohydrates: 29.7 g, Sugar: 26 g, Protein: 5.1 g

---

Vegetarian Taco Salad

Level: Easy
Serves: 4
Carbs: High
Preparation time: 10 minutes

Ingredients:

For the dressing:

- *4 tablespoons olive oil*
- *4 teaspoons chili powder*
- *Juice of 2 limes*
- *4 tablespoons tahini*
- *1 teaspoon maple syrup or agave nectar*

For the salad:

- *2 cups chopped cherry tomatoes*
- *1 cup cooked corn, fresh or frozen*
- *8 cups Romaine lettuce or any greens of your choice*
- *2 cups cooked or canned, drained black beans*
- *1 avocado, peeled, pitted, diced*

Directions:

1. To make the dressing: Add the olive oil, chili powder, lime juice, tahini, and maple syrup into a small bowl and whisk until smooth and well combined. Add a little water to dilute if necessary.
2. Combine the tomatoes, corn, lettuce, black beans, and avocado in a bowl. Drizzle the dressing over the salad. Toss well and serve.

Nutritional value per serving: Calories: 486.7, Fat: 30.7 g, Carbohydrates: 45.9 g, Sugar: 4.5 g, Protein: 14.7 g

Hearty Chickpea and Spinach Stew

Level: Easy
Carbs: High
Number of servings: 2
Preparation time: 10 minutes
Cooking time: 20 minutes

Ingredients:

- *1 ½ cups drained, cooked, or canned chickpeas, rinsed*
- *6 ounces 93% lean ground turkey*
- *2 cloves garlic, peeled, minced, or ¼ teaspoon garlic powder*
- *¼ teaspoon dried oregano*
- *¼ teaspoon fennel seeds, crushed*
- *½ cup chopped onion*
- *2 cups chicken broth*
- *salt to taste*
- *⅛ cup grated parmesan cheese (optional)*
- *2 cups chicken broth*
- *½ tablespoon olive oil*
- *¼ teaspoon crushed red pepper*
- *1 medium carrot, peeled, diced*
- *1 ½ tablespoons tomato paste*
- *⅛ teaspoon ground black pepper*
- *1 ½ cups frozen spinach*

Directions:

1. Place ¾ cup of chickpeas in a bowl and mash with a potato masher.
2. Pour the olive oil into a soup pot and place the pot over medium-high heat.
3. When the oil is hot, add turkey to the pot. Also, add crushed red pepper, oregano, and fennel seeds and stir. As you stir, break the meat into crumbles.
4. Stir on and off until the meat is not pink. Stir in the garlic, carrot, and onion. Cook for a few minutes until you get a nice aroma.
5. Add the tomato paste and stir for ½ a minute.
6. Stir in the broth, whole chickpeas, mashed chickpeas, salt, and pepper. Cook covered until it starts boiling.
7. Reduce the heat, then simmer until the vegetables are cooked. Stir in the spinach.
8. Turn up the heat to medium-high and heat thoroughly. Take it off the heat.
9. Serve in bowls.

Nutritional value per serving: Calories: 401, Fat: 13.4 g, Carbohydrates: 41.3 g, Sugar: 9.6 g, Protein: 32.4 g

Tofu Burrito Bowl

Level: Easy
Carbs: High
Number of servings: 2
Preparation time: 5 minutes
Cooking time: 10 minutes

Ingredients:

- *¼ teaspoon salt or to taste*
- *½ package (from a 14 ounces package) of extra-firm tofu, drained, pressed of excess moisture, chopped*
- *¼ teaspoon chipotle chili powder*
- *¼ teaspoon chili powder*
- *¼ teaspoon paprika*
- *¼ teaspoon pepper*
- *⅛ teaspoon garlic powder*
- *a pinch of cayenne pepper*
- *1 tablespoon olive oil*

For toppings:

- *pico de gallo*
- *cooked or canned black beans or refried beans*
- *chopped red onion*
- *greens like kale, lettuce, spinach, etc.*
- *avocado slices or guacamole*
- *salsa*
- *chopped cilantro*

Directions:

1. To press the tofu of excess moisture, place 2-3 layers of paper towels on a plate. Place the tofu on the paper towels. Place 2-3 layers of paper towels on top of the tofu. Add something heavy on the tofu, like a cold drink can or a heavy pan. Keep it this way for 20 minutes.
2. Heat oil in a skillet and allow it to heat over medium. Add the tofu, chili powder, salt, paprika, chipotle chili powder, pepper, and garlic powder when the oil is hot.
3. Mix it and allow it to cook for a few minutes. Divide the spicy tofu into two bowls. Place desired toppings and serve.

Nutritional value per serving: Calories: 211.1, Fat: 18.6 g, Carbohydrates: 38.8 g, Protein: 10.3 g

Vegan Sandwich

Level: Easy
Serves: 1
Carbs: High
Preparation time: 15 minutes

Ingredients:

For sun-dried tomato basil pesto:

- *2 small cloves garlic, peeled*
- *⅛ cup oil-packed sun-dried tomatoes (about 3 tomatoes)*
- *1 tablespoon fresh lemon juice*
- *½-1 tablespoon extra-virgin olive oil*
- *Freshly ground black pepper to taste*
- *½ cup fresh basil leaves*
- *⅛ cup hulled hemp seeds*
- *1 tablespoon water*
- *⅛ teaspoon salt or to taste*

For the sandwich:

- *2 slices sprouted-grain bread, toasted*
- *1 -2 tablespoons sun-dried tomato basil pesto or to taste*
- *1 thin, round tomato slice*
- *A pinch of red pepper flakes*
- *1 tablespoon hummus*
- *¼ avocado, peeled, pitted, thinly sliced*
- *Lettuce leaves*
- *A pinch of salt*
- *A pinch of pepper*

Directions:

1. To make the pesto: Add the garlic, sun-dried tomatoes, lemon juice, olive oil, pepper, basil, hemp seeds, water, and salt into a blender and blend until smooth.
2. Spread the hummus over one of the slices of toasted bread. On the other slice, spread the pesto.
3. Place the lettuce leaves, tomato, and avocado on any one of the slices of bread. Sprinkle red pepper flakes, salt, and pepper. Cover with the remaining slice of bread. Cut into the desired shape and serve.

Nutritional value per serving: Calories: 503, Fat: 25.6 g, Carbohydrates: 56.4 g, Sugar: 7.3 g, Protein: 17.8 g

Turkey Wrap

Level: Easy
Carbs: High
Serves: 2
Preparation time: 10 minutes
Cooking time: 0 minutes

Ingredients:

- *2 tablespoons mayonnaise*
- *1 green onion, chopped*
- *¾ cup cooked, cubed turkey breast*
- *½ cup halved red grapes*
- *1 tablespoon chopped pecans*
- *1 cup baby spinach*
- *1 tablespoon plain Greek yogurt*
- *⅛ teaspoon salt*
- *⅛ teaspoon pepper*
- *¼ cup thinly sliced celery*
- *1 tablespoon dried cranberries*
- *2 large whole-grain tortillas*

Directions:

1. Mix the mayonnaise, green onion, yogurt, pepper, and salt in a bowl.
2. Add the turkey, grapes, pecans, cranberries, and celery.
3. Place the spinach along the diameter of each tortilla. Divide the turkey mixture equally and place it over the spinach. Wrap like a burrito.
4. You can cut them into halves and serve.

Nutritional value per serving: Calories: 361, Fat: 13.4 g, Carbohydrates: 41.3 g, Sugar: 14.9 g, Protein: 19.1 g

Greek Pita Pockets

Level: Easy
Carbs: High
Serves: 3
Preparation time: 5 minutes
Cooking time: 0 minutes

Ingredients:

- *½ cup crumbled feta cheese*
- *½ cup chopped red onions*
- *1 tablespoon lemon juice*
- *1 ½ cups chopped cucumber*
- *½ cup chopped tomatoes*
- *3 whole-wheat pita bread, halved*

Directions:

1. Firstly, drain off any water from the cucumber or tomatoes.
2. Combine the feta cheese, red onion, lemon juice, cucumber, and tomatoes in a bowl. Mix well.
3. Fill the pita pockets with the salad and serve.

Nutritional value per serving: Calories: 250.6, Fat: 6.2 g, Carbohydrates: 41.9 g, Sugar: 4.1 g, Protein: 10.3 g

Chickpea Quinoa Salad with Hummus Red Pepper Dressing

Level: Easy
Carbs: High
Serves: 2
Preparation time: 10 minutes
Cooking time: 0 minutes

Ingredients:

- *4 tablespoons hummus*
- *⅛ cup chopped roasted red pepper*
- *1 cup cooked quinoa*
- *⅛ cup unsalted sunflower seeds*
- *Salt to taste*
- *2 tablespoons lemon juice*
- *4 cups mixed salad greens*
- *1 cup cooked or canned chickpeas, rinsed*
- *⅛ cup chopped fresh parsley*
- *Pepper to taste*

Directions:

1. Make the dressing by combining the roasted red pepper, lemon juice, and hummus. Add water to dilute the dressing as per your preference.
2. Distribute the salad greens equally among two serving bowls. Place ½ cup each of the quinoa and chickpeas over the greens.
3. Scatter a tablespoon of parsley and sunflower seeds over the chickpeas. Drizzle half the dressing on top in each bowl and serve.

Nutritional value per serving: Calories: 379, Fat: 10.1 g, Carbohydrates: 59.2 g, Sugar: 2.9 g, Protein: 16.2 g

Sweet Potato and Cauliflower Rice Bowl

Level: Easy
Carbs: High
Serves: 2
Preparation time: 10 minutes
Cooking time: 20-25 minutes

Ingredients:

- *½ medium sweet potato, cut into ¼-inch thick slices*
- *Salt to taste*
- *⅛ cup orange juice*
- *¼ cup chopped cilantro, divided*
- *¼ teaspoon ground cumin*
- *2 ½ cups cauliflower florets*
- *½ ripe, firm avocado, peeled, sliced*
- *¼ teaspoon dried oregano*
- *½ can (from a 15-ounce can) of black beans, rinsed, drained*
- *¼ cup Pico de Gallo*
- *4 teaspoons extra-virgin olive oil, divided*
- *Pepper to taste*
- *1 tablespoon lime juice*
- *2 cloves garlic, minced, divided*

Directions:

1. Start by preheating your oven to 350 °F.

2. Drizzle a teaspoon of oil over the sweet potato. Sprinkle salt and pepper and toss well. Spread the sweet potatoes on a baking sheet.
3. Place it in the oven and roast for 14 minutes or until fork tender.
4. Make the dressing by whisking together the lime juice, orange juice, half the garlic, oregano, cumin, salt, and half the cilantro in a bowl.
5. Place the cauliflower florets in the food processor bowl and give short pulses until they resemble rice.
6. Heat three teaspoons of oil in a skillet.
7. When the oil is hot, add the rest of the garlic and stir constantly for a few seconds until you get a pleasant aroma.
8. Stir in the pepper, salt, and cauliflower rice, and mix well. Cook until tender but not overcooked.
9. Turn off the heat. Add remaining cilantro and mix well.
10. Distribute the cauliflower rice into two bowls. Distribute the sweet potato and black beans equally among the bowls.
11. Serve topped with the dressing and Pico de Gallo.

Nutritional value per serving: Calories: 344, Fat: 17.8 g, Carbohydrates: 39 g, Sugar: 8.1 g, Protein: 11 g

Chickpea Salad

Level: Easy
Carbs: High
Serves: 2
Preparation time: 10 minutes
Cooking time: 0 minutes

Ingredients:

- *¼ cup canola mayonnaise*
- *1 tablespoon chopped fresh dill*
- *¼ teaspoon salt*
- *⅛ teaspoon pepper*
- *¼ cup chopped celery*
- *2 tablespoons chopped flat-leaf parsley*
- *¾ teaspoon Dijon mustard*
- *¼ teaspoon smoked paprika*
- *1 can (15 ounces) chickpeas, rinsed, drained*
- *⅛ cup finely chopped shallot*

Directions:

1. Make the dressing in a bowl by stirring the mayonnaise, herbs, paprika, salt, pepper, and mustard.
2. Stir in the celery, chickpeas, and shallots.
3. Serve right away or chill and serve it later.

Nutritional value per serving: Calories: 303, Fat: 9.3 g, Carbohydrates: 36.7 g, Sugar: 3.3 g, Protein: 11.2 g

Green Sandwich

Level: Easy
Serves: 1
Preparation time: 10 minutes

Carbs: High

Cooking time: 0 minutes

Ingredients:

- *¼ cup plain Greek-style yogurt*
- *1 tablespoon chopped fresh tarragon*
- *¼ cup chopped fresh parsley*
- *1 tablespoon chopped fresh chives*
- *½ clove garlic, grated*
- *⅛ cup lemon juice*
- *salt to taste*
- *½ tablespoon chopped, rinsed capers*
- *¾ teaspoon grated lemon zest*
- *½ medium avocado, peeled, cut into 4 slices*
- *2 slices whole-wheat bread (½ inch thick slices)*
- *½ cup thinly sliced cucumber*
- *½ cup spinach or watercress*
- *¼ cup alfalfa sprouts*

Directions:

1. Add the yogurt, herbs, garlic, ½ tablespoon lemon juice, and lemon zest into a bowl and stir well.
2. Add salt and 1 tablespoon of lemon juice to avocado and mix well.
3. Distribute a very generous amount of the herb mixture over each slice of bread.
4. Place the watercress on one bread slice. Layer with cucumber and avocado slices. Spread alfalfa sprouts and cover with the remaining bread slice, with the herb mixture side down.
5. Cut and serve.

Nutritional value per serving: Calories: 387, Fat: 19.9 g, Carbohydrates: 43.4 g, Sugar: 9.7 g, Protein: 15.6 g

Chapter 7: Dinner Recipes

Sage-Rubbed Salmon

Level: Easy
Carbs: Low
Serves: 3
Preparation time: 5-6 minutes
Cooking time: 15-18 minutes

Ingredients:

- 1 tablespoon minced fresh sage
- ½ teaspoon salt
- ¾ pound skin-on salmon filet
- ½ teaspoon garlic powder
- ½ teaspoon freshly ground pepper
- 1 tablespoon olive oil

Directions:

1. Preheat the oven to 375 °F.
2. Combine the sage, salt, garlic powder, and pepper in a small bowl. Sprinkle this mixture on the flesh side of the salmon. Rub it well into it.
3. Now cut the salmon into 3 equal parts.
4. Heat a cast-iron skillet over medium heat and warm the olive oil. When the oil is hot, place the salmon in the skillet with the skin side touching the bottom of the skillet.
5. After cooking the salmon for 5 minutes, turn off the heat and shift the skillet into the preheated oven. Bake until the fish is cooked, roughly around 10 mins.
6. Serve hot.

Nutritional value per serving: Calories: 222, Fat: 14.7 g, Carbohydrates: 1 g, Sugar: 0 g, Protein: 19.4 g

Poached Salmon with Cucumber Sauce

Level: Easy
Carbs: Low
Serves: 2
Preparation time: 5 minutes
Cooking time: 7 minutes
Total time: 12 minutes

Ingredients:

- *½ cup water*
- *½ small onion, sliced*
- *⅛ teaspoon salt or to taste*
- *2 salmon filets (6 ounces each)*
- *¼ cup dry white wine or chicken broth*
- *1 sprig of fresh parsley*
- *2-3 whole peppercorns*
- *Freshly ground black pepper to garnish*

For the sauce:

- *3 tablespoons deseeded, peeled, chopped cucumber*
- *⅛ teaspoon salt or to taste*
- *¼ cup sour cream*
- *½ tablespoon minced onion*
- *⅛ teaspoon dried basil*

Directions:

1. Add the water, onion, salt, wine, parsley, and peppercorns into a pan and mix well.
2. Place it over medium heat and cook uncovered for about 2 minutes or until it begins to boil.
3. Drop the salmon filets into the mixture in the pan with the skin side down. Cover the pan and cook for about 4-5 minutes or until the fish is cooked. If cooked through, it should flake when you pierce it with a fork.
4. In the meantime, prepare the sauce: Add the sour cream, onion, basil, cucumber, and salt into a bowl and mix well.
5. Take out the salmon filets and place them on individual serving plates. Pour 3 tablespoons of sauce over each filet and serve garnished with pepper. The poaching liquid is no longer required.

Nutritional value per serving: Calories: 361.3, Fat: 21 g, Carbohydrates: 3.8 g, Sugar: 2.2 g, Protein: 29.6 g

Parmesan Baked Cod

Level: Easy
Carbs: Low
Serves: 2
Preparation time: 5 minutes
Cooking time: 20 minutes

Ingredients:

- *2 cod filets (4 ounces each)*
- *2 green onions, chopped*
- *½ teaspoon Worcestershire sauce*
- *⅓ cup mayonnaise*

- *⅛ cup grated parmesan cheese*

Directions:

1. Preheat the oven to 400 °F. Coat a baking dish with cooking oil spray.
2. Lay the cod filets in the prepared baking dish.
3. Combine the green onions, Worcestershire sauce, mayonnaise, and parmesan cheese in a bowl.
4. Spread the mixture over the cod.
5. Place it in the oven and bake for 15-20 minutes or until the fish is cooked.

Nutritional value per serving: Calories: 247, Fat: 14.9 g, Carbohydrates: 7 g, Sugar: 1.8 g, Protein: 20.4 g

---

Ground Beef Tacos

Level: Easy
Serves: 4
Preparation time: 10 minutes

Carbs: Low
Cooking time: 10 minutes

Ingredients:

- *½ tablespoon olive oil*
- *1 teaspoon chili powder*
- *¼ teaspoon dried oregano*
- *¼ teaspoon salt*
- *1 tablespoon tomato paste*
- *½ pound lean ground beef*
- *1 teaspoon ground cumin*
- *¼ teaspoon garlic powder*
- *¼ teaspoon ground black pepper*
- *¼ cup water*

To serve: Optional

- *4 whole-grain tortillas or taco shells*
- *Shredded cheese of your choice*
- *Chopped red onions*
- *Finely chopped lettuce*
- *Chopped tomatoes*

Directions:

1. Put the olive oil into a skillet over medium-high. When the oil is hot, place the beef in the skillet. Crumble the meat while stirring.
2. Cook until the meat is brown. Discard any cooked fat from the pan.
3. Stir in the water, spices, and tomato paste. Turn the heat to low and cook until it turns thick.
4. Serve over tortillas or as a filling in the taco shells with any of the suggested serving options.
5. Place the leftover taco meat in the refrigerator. It can be stored for up to 4 days. Freeze in freezer-safe bags for about three months.

Nutritional value per serving: Calories: 144, Fat: 13.5 g, Carbohydrates: 12.3 g, Sugar: 1.2 g, Protein: 13.4 g

Chicken Parmesan

Level: Easy
Carbs: Low
Serves: 3
Preparation time: 15 minutes
Cooking time: 30 minutes

Ingredients:

- *1 ½ pounds chicken breasts*
- *¾ teaspoon dried minced onion*
- *¾ teaspoon dried minced garlic*
- *¾ teaspoon dried oregano*
- *¾ teaspoon dried parsley*
- *¾ teaspoon dried basil*
- *⅛ teaspoon salt*
- *3 ounces shredded mozzarella cheese*
- *½ cup grated parmesan cheese*
- *2 small eggs, beaten*
- *½ cup marinara sauce from a jar*
- *¼ teaspoon freshly ground black pepper*

Directions:

1. First, preheat the oven to 400 °F. Place a sheet of foil on a baking sheet. Spray the foil lightly with some cooking oil spray.
2. Add the parmesan cheese, dried spices, salt, and pepper into a shallow bowl and mix well.
3. Dunk the chicken breast pieces in an egg, one at a time. Shaking off excess egg, dredge the chicken in the cheese mixture and keep it on the baking sheet.
4. When you are done with the breading, pop the baking sheet into the oven and set the timer for 20 to 25 minutes or bake until the inside temperature of the chicken is between 145 °F to 150 °F.
5. Spread the marinara sauce over the chicken. Sprinkle mozzarella on top and bake until the inside temperature of the meat shows 160 °F on the meat thermometer.
6. If you want the cheese browned, set the oven to broil mode and preheat for a few minutes.

Nutritional value per serving: Calories: 398.2, Fat: 16.8 g, Carbohydrates: 6.5 g, Sugar: 1.9 g, Protein: 53.1 g

Chicken Pesto Rolls

Level: Easy
Carbs: Low
Serves: 2
Preparation time: 10 minutes
Cooking time: 30 minutes

Ingredients:

- *2 boneless, skinless chicken breast halves*
- *½ pound medium fresh mushrooms*
- *¼ cup pesto, divided*
- *2 slices low-fat provolone cheese, cut into 2 halves*

Directions:

1. Preheat the oven to 350 °F. Grease a baking dish with cooking spray.
2. Chop some mushrooms and slice the other half.
3. Place the chicken breast on a sheet of plastic wrap. Pound using a meat mallet until it is uniformly about ¼ inch thick.
4. Spoon about 2 tablespoons of pesto over the chicken and spread it evenly. Scatter chopped mushrooms over the chicken. Place half cheese on each chicken.
5. Starting from the shorter end, roll the chicken and fasten it with toothpicks.
6. Scatter the sliced mushrooms on the bottom of the prepared baking dish.
7. Place the chicken rolls over the mushrooms with the seam side down. Now cover the dish with foil.
8. Place the baking dish in the oven and set the timer for about 25 minutes or until the chicken is cooked.
9. Set the oven to broil mode. Remove the foil and spread the remaining pesto over the chicken rolls. Place the remaining cheese slices on top and place them back in the oven. Broil until the cheese melts.
10. Serve.

Nutritional value per serving: Calories: 373.4, Fat: 17.3 g, Carbohydrates: 7.1 g, Sugar: 0.8 g, Protein: 42.4 g

Mediterranean Chicken

Level: Easy
Serves: 2
Preparation time: 10 minutes

Carbs: Low

Cooking time: 20 minutes

Ingredients:

- *2 boneless, skinless chicken breasts*
- *salt to taste*
- *1 ½ teaspoons dried oregano, divided*
- *1 tablespoon minced garlic*
- *pepper to taste*
- *1 tablespoon extra-virgin olive oil*
- *juice of ½ large lemon*
- *½ medium red onion, finely chopped*
- *⅛ cup sliced green onions*
- *Crumbled feta cheese to serve (optional)*
- *¼ cup dry white wine*
- *¼ cup chicken broth*
- *¾ cup diced fresh tomatoes*
- *chopped parsley to garnish*

Directions:

1. Dry the chicken by patting it with paper towels. Score the chicken on either side at 2-3 places.
2. Take some of the garlic and rub it all over the chicken. Place the remaining garlic inside the slits (made by scoring the chicken).
3. Sprinkle salt, ¾ teaspoon oregano, and pepper all over the chicken.
4. Place a cast-iron skillet over medium-high heat and let it heat. Add the olive oil. Once the oil is hot, place the chicken in the skillet and cook until brown on each side.
5. Stir in the white wine. Scrape the pan to dislodge any golden bits. Add broth and lemon juice when the wine reduces to half its original quantity.
6. Scatter the remaining oregano over the chicken and cover the skillet.
7. Turn down the heat to medium and cook for about 5 minutes. Flip the chicken and cook the other side for about 5-6 minutes, until the inside temperature of the chicken shows 165 °F on a meat thermometer.

Nutritional value per serving: Calories: 413.6, Fat: 14.6 g, Carbohydrates: 14.4 g, Sugar: 5.7 g, Protein: 50.5 g

Baked Salsa Chicken

Level: Easy
Carbs: Low
Serves: 2
Preparation time: 10 minutes
Cooking time: 35 minutes

Ingredients:

- *½ tablespoon olive oil*
- *¼ teaspoon ground cumin*
- *¼ teaspoon paprika*
- *salt to taste*
- *½ cup shredded cheddar cheese*
- *freshly ground pepper to taste*
- *2 boneless, skinless chicken breasts*
- *¾ teaspoon chili powder or to taste*
- *¼ teaspoon garlic powder*
- *¾ cup chunky salsa*

Directions:

1. Start by preheating the oven to 375 °F.
2. Place the chicken breast on a sheet of plastic wrap. Pound the chicken using a meat tenderizer until it is uniformly thick.
3. Combine all the spices and salt in a bowl. Sprinkle the spice mixture all over the chicken.
4. Heat a skillet over medium. Add the olive oil. When the oil is hot, place the chicken in the pan and cook until brown on each side. Turn off the heat.
5. Spoon about 4 tablespoons of salsa into a baking dish and spread it evenly.
6. Arrange the chicken over the salsa. Spread the remaining salsa on top.
7. Place the baking dish in the oven to bake for about 30 minutes or until the inside temperature of the chicken shows 165 °F on a meat thermometer.
8. Top with cheese and baking until the cheese melts.
9. Cool for 5 minutes and serve.

Nutritional value per serving: Calories: 307.8, Fat: 14.6 g, Carbohydrates: 7.7 g, Sugar: 3.4 g, Protein: 32.2 g

Golden Apricot-Glazed Turkey Breast

Level: Easy
Carbs: Low
Serves: 7-8
Preparation time: 10 minutes
Cooking time: 45-60 minutes

Ingredients:

- *¼ cup apricot preserves*
- *⅛ teaspoon pepper*
- *2.5 pounds bone-in turkey breast*
- *2 tablespoons balsamic vinegar*
- *⅛ teaspoon salt*

Directions:

1. Firstly, preheat the oven to 325 °F.
2. Add the apricot preserves, salt, pepper, and vinegar into a bowl and mix well.
3. Put the turkey breast on a rack in a roasting pan and place it in the oven.
4. Bake for about 50 to 60 minutes or until the inside temperature of the meat shows 170 °F on a meat thermometer. Brush the apricot mixture over the turkey every 20 minutes while baking.
5. Rest the turkey for 15 minutes. Slice and serve.

Nutritional value per serving: Calories: 235.6, Fat: 7.8 g, Carbohydrates: 8.3 g, Sugar: 4.5 g, Protein: 30.2 g

Turkey Chili

Level: Easy
Carbs: Low
Serves: 3
Preparation time: 10 minutes
Cooking time: 15 minutes

Ingredients:

- *½ tablespoon olive oil*
- *½ tablespoon chili powder*
- *½ teaspoon onion powder*
- *¼ teaspoon pepper*
- *1 teaspoon ground cumin*
- *½ teaspoon salt*
- *½ pound lean ground turkey*
- *1 clove garlic, peeled, minced*
- *½ green bell pepper, deseeded*
- *½ orange or yellow bell pepper, deseeded, diced*
- *½ small onion, diced*
- *½ can (from a 15-ounce can) fire roasted diced tomatoes*
- *1 tablespoon tomato paste*
- *½ can (from a 15-ounce can) of crushed tomatoes*

Directions:

1. Place the olive oil in a pot over medium heat.
2. Place the turkey in the pot when the oil is hot. Stir on and off, breaking the meat. Add all the spices and mix well when the meat is not pink. Stir for a couple of minutes.
3. Add the tomato paste and garlic and mix well. Add the onion and then the bell peppers. Stir for about 3 minutes.
4. Add the diced tomatoes and crushed tomatoes and mix well.
5. When the mixture starts boiling, turn the heat low and cook for 10-12 minutes.
6. Serve with any toppings of your choice.

Nutritional value per serving: Calories: 179, Fat: 8.5 g, Carbohydrates: 10.7 g, Sugar: 5.6 g, Protein: 16.7 g

Spicy Grilled Eggplant

Level: Easy
Carbs: Low
Serves: 4
Preparation time: 10 minutes
Cooking time: 10 minutes

Ingredients:

- *1 small eggplant, cut into ½-inch thick slices*
- *1 tablespoon lime juice*
- *2 tablespoons olive oil*
- *1 ½ teaspoons Cajun seasoning*

Directions:

1. Preheat the oven on medium heat on broil mode.
2. On a baking sheet lined with foil, arrange the eggplant slices.
3. Brush the olive oil over the slices. Season with Cajun seasoning.
4. Place the baking sheet in the oven on the rack about 4 inches below the heating element. Cook for about 4-5 minutes. Flip the eggplant slices over and cook the other side for 4-5 minutes.

Nutritional value per serving: Calories: 88.1, Fat: 6.7 g, Carbs: 7.2 g, Sugar: 2.9 g, Protein: 1 g

Parmesan Roasted Broccoli

Level: Easy
Carbs: Low
Serves: 2
Preparation time: 5 minutes
Cooking time: 20 minutes

Ingredients:

- *1 small head of broccoli (about ½ pound)*
- *¼ teaspoon salt*
- *⅛ teaspoon crushed red pepper flakes*
- *1 tablespoon grated parmesan cheese*
- *1 ½ tablespoons olive oil*
- *¼ teaspoon pepper*
- *2 cloves garlic, thinly sliced*
- *½ teaspoon grated lemon zest*

Directions:

1. Line a sheet of parchment paper on a baking dish and preheat the oven to 425 °F.
2. Cut the broccoli into 4 halves lengthwise (from the head to stem). Place the broccoli pieces in the baking dish.
3. Trickle oil over the broccoli. Season with salt, red pepper flakes, and pepper.
4. Place it in the oven to roast for about 10-12 minutes. Scatter the garlic over the broccoli and continue roasting for 5 minutes. Top with the cheese and roast until the cheese melts.
5. Garnish with lemon zest and serve.

Nutritional value per serving: Calories: 143, Fat: 11 g, Carbs: 9.2 g, Sugar: 1.7 g, Protein: 4.2 g

Meat Loaf

Level: Easy
Carbs: Moderate
Serves: 4
Preparation time: 5-6 minutes
Cooking time: 25-30 minutes

Ingredients:

- *½ cup tomato sauce*
- *½ teaspoon prepared mustard*
- *¼ cup saltine cracker crumbs*
- *1 large egg, lightly beaten*
- *⅛ teaspoon ground black pepper or more to taste*
- *1 pound extra-lean ground beef*
- *⅛ cup brown sugar*
- *½ medium onion, minced*
- *⅛ cup minced green bell pepper*
- *½ teaspoon salt*
- *⅛ teaspoon garlic powder*

Directions:

1. Preheat the oven to 350 °F.
2. Add the brown sugar, tomato sauce, and mustard into a bowl and stir until the sugar dissolves.
3. Add the onion, bell pepper, salt, garlic powder, cracker crumbs, egg, and pepper into a mixing bowl and stir until well incorporated.
4. Stir in the beef and half the tomato sauce mixture. Once the mixture is well combined, shape it into a loaf and place it in a loaf pan lined with foil.
5. Spoon the remaining tomato sauce mixture over the meat. Spread it evenly.
6. Place the loaf pan in the oven and bake for about 30 minutes. The meatloaf should not be pink, and the juices will be released when the meatloaf is cooked. This is another sign to check if the meatloaf is cooked.
7. Remove the meatloaf from the oven and discard any cooked fat from the pan. Let it rest for about 12-15 minutes. Do not cover the pan while it is resting.
8. Cut into four slices and serve.

Nutritional value per serving: Calories: 382, Fat: 19 g, Carbohydrates: 23 g, Sugar: 12 g, Protein: 31 g

Ground Turkey Skillet

Level: Easy
Carbs: Moderate
Serves: 2
Preparation time: 8 minutes
Cooking time: 15 minutes
Total time: 23 minutes

Ingredients:

- *1 medium zucchini, quartered lengthwise, cut into ¾-inch wide slices crosswise*
- *⅛ cup chopped onion*
- *⅛ cup plus ¼ cup canned black beans, rinsed drained*
- *½ large tomato, diced*
- *2 small cloves garlic, peeled, minced*
- *¾ teaspoon ground cumin*
- *⅛ cup water*
- *½ pound 93% lean ground turkey*
- *½ tablespoon tomato paste*
- *⅛ cup plus ½ cup fresh or frozen corn kernels*
- *½ jalapeño, diced*
- *1 tablespoon chopped fresh cilantro + extra to garnish*
- *Salt to taste*
- *Lime wedges to serve (optional)*

Directions:

1. Place a skillet over high heat. Spray the pan with some cooking oil spray.
2. Add the turkey, ½ teaspoon cumin, and salt and stir. As you stir the meat, crumble it into smaller pieces.
3. When the meat is cooked, move the meat to one side of the skillet.
4. Add the tomato paste and onion in the center of the skillet and stir. Cook for about a minute.
5. Stir in the black beans, tomato, garlic, corn, jalapeño, cilantro, and water. Mix the meat as well.
6. Stir in ¼ teaspoon cumin, zucchini, and salt. Cover the pan and turn down the heat to low. Cook for a few minutes until the zucchini is crisp and tender.
7. Sprinkle some cilantro and add lime wedges and serve.

Nutritional value per serving: Calories: 266, Fat: 8.5 g, Carbohydrates: 22.5 g, Sugar: 4.3 g, Protein: 28 g

Lemon-Broccoli Pasta with Parmesan

Level: Easy
Serves: 2
Preparation time: 8 minutes
Total time: 23 minutes

Carbs: Moderate

Cooking time: 15 minutes

Ingredients:

- *3 tablespoons grated parmesan cheese*
- *1 tablespoon extra-virgin olive oil*
- *¾ cup low-sodium vegetable broth or chicken broth*
- *5 ounces frozen broccoli florets, thawed, chopped*
- *1 clove garlic, peeled, minced*
- *¾ cup + ⅛ cup water*
- *4 ounces whole-wheat rotini pasta or farfalle pasta*
- *½ tablespoon grated lemon zest*
- *¼ teaspoon ground black pepper*
- *½ medium shallot, minced*
- *¼ teaspoon salt*
- *2 teaspoons lemon juice or more to taste*

Directions:

1. Pour the olive oil into a saucepan and place it over medium heat. Add the shallot to the oil and cook until it is slightly soft.
2. Add the garlic and stir for a few seconds.
3. Add in the water, broth, pasta, lemon zest, and salt, and pepper.
4. Put on a lid and cook until it starts boiling. Reduce the heat to medium and simmer until the pasta is nearly al dente. Add the broccoli and cook for a few minutes.
5. Take off the heat and add the lemon juice and parmesan cheese. Mix well.
6. Serve hot.

Nutritional value per serving: Calories: 213, Fat: 10.2 g, Carbohydrates: 23.9 g, Sugar: 1.9 g, Protein: 9.3 g

Warm Chicken Salad with Peas and Polenta

Level: Easy
Serves: 2
Preparation time: 10 minutes
Carbs: Moderate
Cooking time: 15 minutes

Ingredients:

- *2 teaspoons extra-virgin olive oil, divided*
- *½ pound cooked chicken, diced or shredded*
- *¼ cup nonfat plain Greek yogurt*
- *½ tube (16-18 ounces tube) polenta, cut into 4 rounds*
- *½ pound frozen peas, thawed*
- *¼ cup pesto*

Directions:

1. Add 1 teaspoon of olive oil to a nonstick pan and let it heat over medium heat. Swirl the pan to spread the oil.
2. Place the polenta slices in the pan. Cook on both sides for 3-4 minutes each.
3. Remove from the pan and place 2 polenta rounds on each plate.
4. Add 1 teaspoon of olive oil to the same pan. Add the peas and chicken into the pan and heat thoroughly.
5. Turn off the heat. Add the yogurt and pesto and mix well.

Nutritional value per serving: Calories: 534, Fat: 21.2g, Carbs: 33.4g, Sugar: 8.1g, Protein: 47.8g

---

Brown Rice and Veggies

Level: Easy
Serves: 2
Preparation time: 10 minutes
Carbs: Moderate
Cooking time: 20-25 minutes

Ingredients:

- *1 teaspoon extra-virgin olive oil*
- *4 ounces white button mushrooms, sliced*
- *Salt to taste*
- *½ cup brown rice, rinsed, drained*
- *½ cup frozen peas, thawed*
- *⅛ cup grated parmesan cheese to serve*
- *½ small onion, chopped*
- *2 small cloves garlic, minced*
- *¼ teaspoon pepper or to taste*
- *1 cup low-sodium vegetable broth or chicken broth*
- *2 cups loosely packed baby spinach*

Directions:

1. Add the olive oil to a pot and place it over medium heat.
2. Add the mushrooms and onion, when the oil gets hot and stir. Cook until the mushrooms are tender.

3. Stir in salt, garlic, and pepper.
4. Stir in the brown rice. Stir for a few minutes until the rice is well coated with the oil.
5. Pour the chicken broth into the pot and stir. When it starts boiling, put a lid on the pot and reduce the heat. Cook until nearly dry and the rice turns al dente.
6. Stir in the spinach and peas. Now turn off the heat. Let the pot remain covered for 5-8 minutes.
7. Mix well. Garnish with the parmesan cheese and serve.

Nutritional value per serving: Calories: 211.3, Fat: 5.2 g, Carbs: 25.6 g, Sugar: 5.6 g, Protein: 17 g

HIGH-CARB RECIPES

Linguine Skillet

Level: Easy
Carbs: High
Serves: 1
Preparation time: 5 minutes
Cooking time: 20 minutes
Total time: 25 minutes

Ingredients:

- *2 ounces of uncooked whole-wheat linguine*
- *½ plum tomato cut into 1-inch cubes*
- *1 teaspoon lemon juice*
- *⅛ teaspoon pepper or to taste*
- *½ tablespoon minced fresh parsley*
- *2 bacon strips, cut into 1 ½ inch pieces*
- *½ clove garlic, minced*
- *Salt to taste*
- *1 tablespoon grated parmesan cheese*

Directions:

1. Cook the pasta as per the instructions given on the package.
2. In the meantime, place a skillet over medium heat. When the pan is hot, add the bacon and cook until it turns crispy.
3. Line a plate with 2-3 layers of paper towels. Remove the bacon, retaining about half a teaspoon of the bacon fat and discard the remaining.
4. Add the garlic to the pan and cook for a few seconds until you get a nice aroma.
5. Stir in the tomatoes and cook for about a minute. Add the bacon, salt, lemon juice, and pepper and mix well.
6. Add the linguine and toss well. Add parsley and the cheese and toss well.

Nutritional value per serving: Calories: 313, Fat: 10.9g, Carbs: 45.6g, Sugar: 2.2g, Protein: 13.4g

Black Bean Fajita Skillet

Level: Easy
Carbs: High
Serves: 4
Preparation time: 10 minutes
Cooking time: 12-15 minutes

Ingredients:

- *2 tablespoons olive oil*
- *2 cans (15 ounces each) of black beans, drained, rinsed*
- *½ teaspoon salt or to taste*
- *2 packages (12 ounces each) of sliced fajita vegetables*
- *1 teaspoon salt-free Southwest-style seasoning blend*
- *½ cup shredded cheddar cheese (optional)*

Directions:

1. Heat a skillet over medium heat and heat some olive oil in it. When the oil is hot, add the fajita vegetables to the skillet and stir on and off until the vegetables are tender.
2. Add the black beans, salt, and seasoning blend and mix well. Heat thoroughly.
3. Distribute the mixture equally among four bowls. Sprinkle 2 tablespoons of cheese on top in each bowl and serve.

Nutritional value per serving: Calories: 312.1, Fat: 6.8 g, Carbohydrates: 47.3 g, Sugar: 7.8 g, Protein: 13.4 g

Mashed Sweet Potatoes

Level: Easy
Carbs: High
Serves: 3
Preparation time: 10 minutes
Cooking time: 25 minutes

Ingredients:

- *3 medium sweet potatoes, peeled, cubed*
- *¼ cup butter, chopped into chunks, softened*
- *6 tablespoons warm, low-fat milk or more if required*
- *6 tablespoons maple syrup*

Directions:

1. Boil a pot of water with about a teaspoon of salt added to it. Add the sweet potatoes to the pot when the water comes to a boil.
2. Bring the heat to medium-low and cook until the sweet potatoes are soft. Drain off the water.
3. Mash the sweet potatoes in a bowl. Add about 4 tablespoons of milk and mix well.
4. Add the butter and maple syrup and mix well.

Nutritional value per serving: Calories: 352.3, Fat: 15.9g, Carbs: 51.7g, Sugar: 31.2g, Protein: 3.2g

Vegan Burrito Bowls

Level: Easy
Carbs: High
Serves: 3
Preparation time: 10 minutes
Cooking time: 20 minutes
Total time: 30 minutes

Ingredients:

- *½ large red bell pepper, cut into small squares*
- *1 medium sweet potato, peeled, cut into small cubes*
- *½½ medium red onion, diced*
- *½ medium zucchini, cut into small cubes*
- *1 ½ cups drained, canned, or cooked black beans, rinsed*
- *1 medium jalapeno, deseeded, finely chopped*
- *½ tablespoon extra-virgin olive oil*
- *½ teaspoon ground cumin*
- *½ teaspoon chili powder*
- *½ teaspoon paprika*
- *salt and pepper to taste*
- *juice of ½ lime*
- *¼ cup chopped fresh cilantro*
- *toppings of your choice like avocado, tomatoes, lettuce, etc.*

Directions:

1. Preheat the oven to 400 °F.
2. Add the zucchini, sweet potato, onion, jalapeño, bell pepper, and oil to a baking pan and mix well.
3. Sprinkle the spices and seasonings on the vegetables and mix well.
4. Roast the veggies in the oven for 20 minutes or until the sweet potatoes are well cooked.
5. Mix the vegetables once while baking. Add the lime juice and black beans.
6. Divide everything in three bowls and serve with any toppings if desired.

Nutritional value per serving: Calories: 221.2, Fat: 2.3 g, Carbohydrates: 39.8 g, Sugar: 5.6 g, Protein: 9 g

Spaghetti with Spinach Pesto

Level: Easy
Carbs: High
Serves: 2-3
Preparation time: 10 minutes
Cooking time: 25 minutes

Ingredients:

- *1 cup packed baby spinach*
- *½ cup thinly sliced new potatoes or baby potatoes*
- *¼ cup pesto*
- *¼ teaspoon salt*
- *4 ounces whole-wheat spaghetti*
- *½ pound green beans, trimmed, cut into 1-inch pieces*
- *Freshly ground pepper to taste*

Directions:

1. Blanch the spinach in a pot of boiling water for about 45 seconds. Lift the spinach with a sieve and place it in a blender.
2. Add the potatoes and spaghetti into the boiling water and cook until the spaghetti is half cooked.
3. Add the green beans into the boiling water and cook the spaghetti to al dente. Retain about ½ cup of the boiling liquid and drain off the remaining water. Add the spaghetti back into the pot.
4. Add the pesto, salt, pepper, and about ¼ cup of the retained water into the blender and blend with the spinach until you get a smooth puree.
5. Pour the blended mixture into the pot. Place the pot over medium heat and heat thoroughly, stirring on and off.
6. If you want to dilute the sauce, add the remaining cooked water.

Nutritional value per serving: Calories: 331, Fat: 11.2 g, Carbohydrates: 47 g, Sugar: 3.3 g, Protein: 13.4 g

---

Chicken and Vegetable Curry Couscous

Level: Easy
Carbs: High
Serves: 3
Preparation time: 10 minutes
Cooking time: 15 minutes

Ingredients:

- *½ tablespoon butter*
- *½ package (from a 16 ounces package) of frozen vegetables of your choice*
- *½ package (from a 5.7 ounces package) curry flavored couscous*
- *½ pound boneless, skinless chicken breasts cut into strips*
- *2/3 cup water*
- *¼ cup raisins*

Directions:

1. Place a heavy skillet over medium-high heat and melt the butter in it.
2. Cook the chicken in the melted butter until it is no longer pink.
3. Stir in the vegetables and water. Add half a package of couscous seasoning that comes along with the couscous.
4. When it starts boiling, add raisins and couscous and stir. Turn off the heat.
5. Cover the skillet and let it rest for 5-6 minutes. Loosen the couscous grains using a fork.
6. Serve hot.

Nutritional value per serving: Calories: 273.6, Fat: 3.4 g, Carbohydrates: 39.1 g, Sugar: 8.9 g, Protein: 21 g

One-Pot Chicken, Carrots, and Lentils Meal

Level: Easy **Carbs:** High
Serves: 3
Preparation time: 15 minutes **Cooking time:** 40 minutes

Ingredients:

- *¾ pound boneless, skinless chicken thighs*
- *¼ teaspoon salt*
- *2 small cloves garlic, crushed*
- *½ small carrot, peeled, finely chopped*
- *2 small carrots, peeled, trimmed*
- *½ medium tomato, coarsely chopped*
- *1 cup vegetable broth*
- *4 cherry tomatoes*
- *4 tablespoons balsamic vinegar divided*
- *¼ teaspoon pepper*
- *½ small onion, finely chopped*
- *1 ½ small onions, sliced*
- *½ celery stalk, finely chopped*
- *3.5 ounces dried lentils, rinsed, soaked in water for an hour if possible*
- *1 bay leaf*
- *2 teaspoons extra-virgin olive oil, divided plus extra to drizzle*

Directions:

1. Score the chicken at a few places.
2. Add 2 ½ tablespoons of vinegar, pepper, and ⅛ teaspoon of salt into a shallow bowl and mix well.
3. Place the chicken thighs in the bowl and turn them around to coat well. Keep it aside for now.
4. Add 1 teaspoon of olive oil into a pot and let it heat over medium heat.
5. Add the finely chopped onion and garlic and cook for a couple of minutes.
6. Stir in the celery, tomatoes, and finely chopped carrots, and cook for a few minutes.
7. Stir in the drained lentils. Stir for about a minute. Add a bay leaf and broth and stir.
8. When it starts boiling, turn down the heat and simmer until the lentils are cooked. If there is no broth in the pot and the lentils aren't cooked, boil some broth and add to the pot.
9. While the lentils are simmering, place a pan over medium heat. Add a teaspoon of olive oil and let it heat. Add the chicken into the pan along with the vinegar. Cook until brown all over. When the chicken is cooked on one side, add the whole carrots into the pan and cook until the chicken is tender.
10. Move the chicken and carrots to any one side of the pan.
11. Add the sliced onions to the center of the pan. Cook for a couple of minutes. Add the tomatoes and lentils, then thoroughly whisk all of the ingredients in the pan.
12. Transfer into a bowl. Trickle some olive oil on top and serve.

Nutritional value per serving: Calories: 363, Fat: 6.4 g, Carbohydrates: 41 g, Sugar: 9.9 g, Protein: 33.4 g

Salmon and Sweet Potato Grain Bowls

Level: Easy
Serves: 4
Preparation time: 15 minutes
Carbs: High
Cooking time: 30 minutes

Ingredients:

- *4 tablespoons extra-virgin olive oil*
- *½ teaspoon salt*
- *4 salmon filets (4 ounces each), skinless*
- *2 cups warm, cooked farro*
- *2 tablespoons harissa*
- *2 large sweet potatoes, peeled, cut into 1-inch cubes*
- *4 cups baby spinach*

Directions:

1. Start by preheating the oven to 425° F. Grease a rimmed baking sheet with some cooking spray.
2. Add the harissa, olive oil, and salt into a bowl and mix well. Stir in the sweet potato cubes.
3. Spread the potatoes on the baking sheet and place them in the oven. Roast for 20 minutes.
4. Add the salmon into the bowl in which the sweet potatoes sat, and mix the salmon filets around in any harissa mixture in the bowl.
5. Place the fish and potatoes on the baking sheet, and roast until cooked.
6. In the meantime, combine the spinach and farro.
7. Distribute the farro mixture among four bowls. Distribute the sweet potatoes among the bowls. Place a salmon filet in each bowl and serve.

Nutritional value per serving: Calories: 663, Fat: 28 g, Carbohydrates: 62 g, Sugar: 8.9 g, Protein: 37 g

Pasta with Tuna

Level: Easy
Serves: 2
Preparation time: 10 minutes
Carbs: High
Cooking time: 30 minutes

Ingredients:

- *4 ounces whole-wheat spaghetti*
- *1 teaspoon grated lemon zest*
- *1 tablespoon lemon juice or to taste*
- *¼ teaspoon pepper*
- *⅛ cup loosely packed fresh dill*
- *1 ½ cups plus ⅛ cup water*
- *¼ cup olives, pitted*
- *¼ teaspoon salt or to taste*
- *1 can (5 ounces) unsalted tuna, drained, flaked*
- *1 tablespoon extra-virgin olive oil*

Directions:

1. Add the spaghetti, lemon zest, salt, pepper, water, olives, and lemon juice into a pan and place it over high heat.
2. When the water starts boiling, turn down the heat and cook until the pasta is al dente and hardly any water remains in the pan.
3. Turn off the heat. Add the tuna, olive oil, and dill and mix well.
4. Serve.

Nutritional value per serving: Calories: 381, Fat: 14.3 g, Carbohydrates: 41.2 g, Sugar: 2.2 g, Protein: 21 g

Goat Cheese and Broccoli Pasta

Level: Easy
Carbs: High
Serves: 4
Preparation time: 5 minutes
Cooking time: 15 minutes

Ingredients:

- *8 ounces chickpea cavatappi pasta*
- *4 cups broccoli florets*
- *4 ounces garlic and herb-flavored goat cheese*
- *salt to taste*
- *pepper to taste*

Directions:

1. Cook the pasta as per the directions on the package. During the last three minutes of cooking, add the broccoli.
2. Retain some of the cooked water and drain off the remaining water.
3. Add the pasta back into the pot.
4. Stir in the goat cheese. Place the pot over medium heat and cook until the cheese melts. Add salt and pepper to taste.
5. Serve hot.

Nutritional value per serving: Calories: 293, Fat: 9.1 g, Carbohydrates: 36.7 g, Sugar: 6.4 g, Protein: 21.3 g

One Pot of Ground Turkey Pasta

Level: Easy
Serves: 3
Preparation time: 5 minutes

Carbs: High
Cooking time: 20-25 minutes

Ingredients:

- *½ tablespoon extra-virgin olive oil*
- *½ tablespoon Italian herb seasoning*
- *½ onion, diced*
- *½ large carrot, diced*
- *12.8 ounces ground lean turkey (93% lean)*
- *¼ teaspoon pepper*
- *1 large stalk of celery, diced*
- *2 cloves garlic, minced*
- *½ tablespoon soy sauce or tamari*
- *1 ½ tablespoons nutritional yeast or parmesan cheese*
- *½ can (from a 15-ounce can) of diced tomatoes*
- *Red chili flakes to garnish*
- *Fresh herbs of your choice to garnish*
- *½ tablespoon balsamic vinegar*
- *5 ounces dried, gluten-free penne pasta*
- *1 ¼ cups chicken stock*
- *1 cup chopped spinach*

Directions:

1. Add ½ tablespoon of oil into a skillet (that has a fitting lid) and place it over medium-high heat.
2. Add the turkey to the hot oil and add salt, pepper, and Italian herbs.
3. Stir on and off until the meat no longer looks pink. Crumble the meat while stirring.
4. Stir in the garlic, celery, onion, and carrot. When the turkey is brown, stir in the vinegar and soy sauce.
5. After about a minute, add the penne and tomatoes. Pour the stock into the skillet and mix well. Press the mixture onto the bottom of the skillet so that the mixture is immersed in the stock.
6. Cook on medium-low heat until it starts simmering. Now place the lid on the skillet and simmer until the pasta is cooked. Remove the skillet from heat.
7. Place the spinach on top and cover the skillet for a few minutes. Now give the pasta a good stir. Add some salt and pepper if required.
8. Garnish with fresh herbs and serve hot.

Nutritional value per serving: Calories: 423, Fat: 13.3 g, Carbohydrates: 46.6 g, Sugar: 2.3 g, Protein: 32.2 g

Couscous with Shrimp and Peas

Level: Easy
Carbs: High
Serves: 2
Preparation time: 10 minutes
Cooking time: 20 minutes

Ingredients:

- *½ pound large shrimp with tail on, peeled, deveined*
- *½ small onion, chopped*
- *½ bell pepper chopped*
- *½ cup uncooked couscous*
- *¼ cup frozen peas*
- *½ tablespoon olive oil*
- *2 cloves garlic, minced*
- *⅛ cup raisins*
- *1 cup chicken broth*
- *½ teaspoon ground cumin*
- *Salt to taste*
- *Pepper to taste*
- *½ teaspoon smoked paprika*
- *⅛ cup chopped pistachios*

Directions:

1. Place the shrimp in a bowl. Sprinkle the paprika, cumin, pepper, and salt over the shrimp and toss well.
2. Add the olive oil into a skillet and place it over high heat. Wait for the oil to smoke. Place the shrimp in the pan in a single layer. Cook for 1-2 minutes. Flip sides and cook the other side for 1-2 minutes or until they turn pink and add them to a bowl when done.
3. Now add the bell pepper and onion into the skillet and stir. Cook until the onion turns pink.
4. Stir in the garlic and raisins. Stir constantly for about a minute.
5. Stir in the couscous and broth. When the mixture starts boiling, boil the heat and cook until dry.
6. Add the peas and cook for about 2 minutes or until the peas are heated thoroughly.
7. Turn off the heat. Stir in the shrimp. Sprinkle parsley and pistachios on top and serve.

Nutritional value per serving: Calories: 433, Fat: 11 g, Carbohydrates: 49 g, Sugar: 4.3 g, Protein: 34 g

Chickpea Tortilla Soup

Level: Easy
Carbs: High
Serves: 4
Preparation time: 10 minutes
Cooking time: 20-25 minutes

Ingredients:

- *½ tablespoon olive oil*
- *2 cloves garlic, minced*
- *⅛ teaspoon pepper or to taste*
- *½ cup red quinoa rinsed*
- *½ can (from a 15-ounce can) of unsalted black beans, rinsed drained*
- *1 can (15 ounces) of unsalted chickpeas, rinsed, drained*
- *½ cup fresh or frozen corn*
- *1 ½ medium tomatoes, chopped*
- *½ medium red onion, chopped*
- *½-1 jalapeño pepper, deseeded, chopped (optional)*
- *4 cups vegetable broth*
- *a handful of fresh cilantro chopped*

To serve: Optional

- *chopped avocado*
- *crushed tortilla chips*
- *chopped cilantro*
- *lime wedges*
- *any other toppings*

Directions:

1. Add the olive oil into a Dutch oven and place it over medium-high heat. When the oil is hot, add the onion, garlic, and jalapeño and mix well.
2. Stir on and off until the onions are soft.
3. Stir in the quinoa and broth. When it starts boiling, boil the heat to low and let it simmer until the quinoa is cooked.
4. Stir in the black beans, chickpeas, tomatoes, cilantro, and corn. Let it simmer for about 10 minutes.
5. Serve with any of the suggested serving options if desired or it can be enjoyed without any toppings too.

Nutritional value per serving: Calories: 289, Fat: 5.7 g, Carbohydrates: 48 g, Sugar: 4.5 g, Protein: 13 g

Chapter 8: Snack Recipes

Mini Cheese Balls

Level: Easy
Carbs: Low
Serves: 9
Preparation time: 15 minutes
Cooking time: 0 minutes plus chilling time

Ingredients:

For the cheese balls:

- *1 cup shredded sharp cheddar cheese*
- *4 ounces cream cheese, softened*

For dredging: Optional

- *Paprika*
- *Minced fresh rosemary*
- *Toasted sesame seeds*

To serve: Optional

- *Halved rye crisps*
- *Rolled tortilla chips*

Directions:

1. Add the cream cheese and cheddar cheese into a bowl and mix well.
2. Make 18 balls of the mixture.
3. Dredge the balls in paprika, rosemary, and sesame seeds. You can dredge them separately in each of the paprika, sesame seeds, or rosemary or combine the spices in a bowl and dredge the balls in that.
4. Place the balls on a plate. Insert a rye crisp or rolled tortilla chip in each ball and serve.

Nutritional value per serving: Calories: 93.4, Fat: 7.8 g, Carbohydrates: 2.1 g, Sugar: 0 g, Protein: 4.2 g

---

Spicy Mixed Nuts

Level: Easy
Carbs: Low
Serves: 6
Preparation time: 5 minutes
Cooking time: 10 minutes

Ingredients:

- *1 ½ tablespoons butter*
- *⅛ teaspoon Worcestershire sauce*
- *⅛ teaspoon paprika or more to taste*

- *8 ounces mixed nuts*
- *¼ teaspoon salt or more to taste*

Directions:

1. Place a skillet over low heat. Add the butter and wait for it to melt.
2. Add the mixed nuts and Worcestershire sauce into the melted butter and mix well.
3. Cook for 5-7 minutes, and stir often. When no liquid is left in the pan, turn off the heat.
4. Transfer the nuts to a plate lined with paper towels. Once they cool, place them in a bowl.
5. Sprinkle paprika and salt over the nuts. Mix well.

Nutritional value per serving: Calories: 226.1, Fat: 18.9 g, Carbohydrates: 9.7 g, Sugar: 1.9 g, Protein: 6.7 g

Spicy Lemon Chicken Kabobs

Level: Moderate
Carbs: Low
Serves: 3
Preparation time: 10 minutes plus marinating time
Cooking time: 10 minutes

Ingredients:

- *⅛ cup lemon juice*
- *1 ½ tablespoons white wine*
- *½ teaspoon minced fresh rosemary or ⅛ teaspoon dried rosemary, crushed*
- *1 lemon halved*
- *2 tablespoons olive oil, divided*
- *¾ teaspoon crushed red pepper flakes*
- *¾ pound boneless, skinless chicken breasts cut into bite-size pieces*
- *Finely chopped chives to garnish*

Directions:

1. Add the rosemary, wine, 1 ½ tablespoons of oil, and red pepper flakes into a bowl and mix well.
2. Stir in the chicken. Place it covered in the refrigerator for 2-3 hours.
3. Before grilling, soak the wooden skewers in water for 30 minutes. Remove the chicken from the fridge, discard the marinade, and fix the chicken onto three skewers.
4. Place the skewered chicken in a preheated grill. Cover the grill and cook over medium heat for about 6 minutes. Turn the skewers over and cook for another 5-6 minutes or until the chicken is cooked.
5. While grilling the chicken, grill the lemon halves until light brown.
6. On a serving platter, arrange the chicken skewers. Squeeze the juice from the lemon over the chicken. Trickle ½ tablespoon of olive oil over the chicken. Garnish with chives and serve.

Nutritional value per serving: Calories: 181.7, Fat: 8.2 g, Carbohydrates: 2.1 g, Sugar: 1.1 g, Protein: 22.3 g

Buffalo Chicken Wings

Level: Moderate **Carbs:** Low
Serves: 4
Preparation time: 5 minutes **Cooking time:** 50 minutes

Ingredients:

- *2 pounds chicken wings, cut into drumettes and flats*
- *¼ teaspoon salt*
- *Cracked pepper to taste*
- *½ tablespoon baking powder*
- *1 teaspoon garlic powder*

For the buffalo sauce:

- *¼ cup Frank's original red hot sauce*
- *⅛ cup unsalted butter, melted*
- *½-1 tablespoon honey or brown sugar*

For the blue cheese dip:

- *3 tablespoons sour cream*
- *1 clove garlic, minced*
- *A pinch of salt*
- *¼ cup crumbled blue cheese softened*
- *⅛ cup mayonnaise*
- *½ tablespoon lemon juice*
- *Cracked black pepper to taste*

To serve:

- *Celery sticks*

Directions:

1. Place the rack in the upper third position in the oven.
2. Preheat the oven to 450 °F. Arrange a sheet of foil on a baking sheet.
3. Place a wire rack on the baking sheet.
4. Dry the wings with paper towels. Place chicken wings in a bowl.
5. Add the baking powder and seasonings to a bowl and mix well. Sprinkle this mixture over the wings.
6. Place the wings on the rack without overlapping.
7. Please place it in the oven and set the timer for about 50 minutes, flipping the sides after 30 minutes of baking. They should be baked until crisp and brown.
8. Make the buffalo sauce by combining honey, butter, and hot sauce.
9. Make the cheese sauce dip by combining the sour cream, garlic, salt, blue cheese, mayonnaise, lemon juice, and pepper.
10. Transfer the baked wings to a bowl. Spread the sauce over the wings and toss well.
11. Serve the buffalo wings with celery sticks and cheese dip.

Nutritional value per serving: Calories: 411, Fat: 33 g, Carbohydrates: 2.8 g, Sugar: 1.7 g, Protein: 24.3 g

Tortilla Rolls

Level: Easy
Serves: 4
Preparation time: 5 minutes
Carbs: Low
Cooking time: 0 minutes

Ingredients:
- *2 tablespoons fat-free cream cheese*
- *4 tablespoons salsa*
- *¼ teaspoon chili powder*
- *4 tablespoons low-fat cheddar cheese*
- *⅛ cup chopped greens of green onion*
- *2 whole wheat tortillas*

Directions:
1. Add both the cheddar and cream cheese in a bowl and mix it.
2. Stir in the salsa, chili powder, and green onions.
3. Divide the mixture equally and spread over the tortillas.
4. With the seam side out, roll the tortilla. Cut into four equal pieces and serve.

Nutritional value per serving: Calories: 92.9, Fat: 1.9 g, Carbohydrates: 12.4 g, Sugar: 1.9 g, Protein: 5.8 g

Caprese Salad Kabobs

Level: Super Easy
Serves: 6
Preparation time: 5 minutes
Carbs: Low
Cooking time: 0 minutes

Ingredients:
- *12 grape tomatoes*
- *12 fresh basil leaves*
- *1 teaspoon balsamic vinegar*
- *6 cherry-sized fresh mozzarella cheese balls*
- *1 tablespoon olive oil*

Directions:
1. Take six appetizer skewers or small wooden skewers and fix a tomato into each skewer, followed by a basil leaf. Next, insert a cheese ball in each, followed by a basil leaf. Finally, insert a tomato and place it over a plate.
2. Combine the vinegar and olive oil in a bowl. Drizzle this mixture over the kabobs and serve.

Nutritional value per serving: Calories: 43.4, Fat: 3.8 g, Carbohydrates: 2.2 g, Sugar: 1.2 g, Protein: 0.9 g

Savory Date and Pistachio Bites

Level: Easy
Serves: 16
Preparation time: 10 minutes
Carbs: Low
Cooking time: 0 minutes

Ingredients:

- *1 cup pitted dates*
- *½ cup golden raisins*
- *⅛ teaspoon pepper*
- *½ cup unsalted, shelled pistachios*
- *½ teaspoon ground fennel seeds*

Directions:

1. Place the dates, raisins, pepper, fennel, and pistachios in the food processor bowl and process until very finely chopped.
2. Transfer the mixture to a bowl. Make 16 equal portions of the mixture and shape into balls.
3. Store in the refrigerator until use.

Nutritional value per serving: Calories: 67.8, Fat: 1.9 g, Carbohydrates: 12.3 g, Sugar: 11.1 g, Protein: 1 g

Banana and Chocolate Mini Muffins

Level: Moderate
Serves: 12
Preparation time: 15 minutes
Carbs: Low
Cooking time: 30 minutes

Ingredients:

- *¾ cup rolled oats*
- *⅛ teaspoon baking soda*
- *½ teaspoon baking powder*
- *⅛ teaspoon salt*
- *½ cup mashed overripe banana*
- *1 ½ tablespoons canola oil*
- *¼ cup mini chocolate chips*
- *1 large egg*
- *3 tablespoons packed brown sugar*
- *½ teaspoon vanilla extract*

Directions:

1. Start by preheating the oven to 350 °F. Grease a mini muffin pan (12-count) with cooking oil spray. Place disposable liners if desired. I recommend them.
2. Finely grind the oats in a blender. Add the baking soda, salt, and baking powder and process until well combined.
3. Crack the egg into the blender. Add the brown sugar, banana, vanilla, and olive oil and blend until you get a smooth batter.
4. Pour the batter into a bowl. Add the chocolate chips and stir.

5. Ladle the batter up to ¾ of the muffin cups. Transfer the muffin pan into the oven and bake for 15-16 minutes. Insert a toothpick in a muffin to check if it is cooked through. If any batter is stuck on the toothpick, you will need to bake for 5-7 minutes longer. Then, take it out.
6. Take the muffin pan out of the oven and cool for a few minutes in the pan itself.
7. Take the muffins out of the pan and cool on a wire rack.
8. Serve.

Nutritional value per serving: Calories: 77.8, Fat: 3.4 g, Carbohydrates: 13 g, Sugar: 5.6 g, Protein: 1 g

MODERATE-CARB RECIPES

Trail Mix

Level: Easy
Carbs: Moderate
Serves: 7-8
Preparation time: 5 minutes
Cooking time: 0 minutes

Ingredients:

- *½ cup salted pumpkin seeds or pepitas*
- *½ cup unsalted sunflower seeds*
- *½ cup dried apricots*
- *½ cup almonds*
- *½ cup walnut halves*
- *½ cup dark chocolate chips*

Directions:

1. Combine the seeds, nuts, apricots, and chocolate chips in an airtight container and store at room temperature.

Nutritional value per serving: Calories: 337, Fat: 23 g, Carbohydrates: 21.2 g, Sugar: 13.1 g, Protein: 12.4 g

Peanut Butter Energy Balls

Level: Easy
Serves: 16
Preparation time: 15 minutes plus chilling time

Carbs: Moderate
Cooking time: 0 minutes

Ingredients:

- *1 ⅓ cups natural peanut butter*
- *3 tablespoons honey*
- *½ cup flaxseeds (optional)*
- *2 cups old-fashioned oats plus extra to dredge*
- *½ cup mini chocolate chips plus extra to dredge*

Directions:

1. In a bowl, combine the peanut butter, honey, flaxseeds, oats, and chocolate chips.
2. Grease your hands with a little oil. Make 16 equal balls.
3. Dredge the balls in some oats and chocolate chips on a plate and store them in an airtight container in the refrigerator.

Nutritional value per serving: Calories: 337.8, Fat: 21.2 g, Carbohydrates: 26.3 g, Sugar: 5.6 g, Protein: 9.9 g

Fruit Kabobs with Cream Cheese Dip

Level: Easy
Serves: 3
Preparation time: 10 minutes

Carbs: Moderate
Cooking time: 0 minutes

Ingredients:

- *3 ounces cream cheese, softened*
- *3 tablespoons sour cream*
- *6 fresh strawberries, hulled*
- *6 fresh pineapple cubes*
- *3 tablespoons confectioners' sugar*
- *⅛ teaspoon almond extract*
- *6 green grapes*

Directions:

1. To make the dip: Add the cream cheese, sour cream, confectioners' sugar, and almond extract into a bowl and use an electric hand mixer to blend until smooth.
2. Cover the bowl and chill until ready to serve.
3. Take 6 appetizer skewers or wooden skewers and fix the fruits on them in a colorful manner.
4. Place the skewers on a plate and chill until ready to serve.
5. Serve fruit kabobs with dip.

Nutritional value per serving: Calories: 183.7, Fat: 12.8g, Carbs: 17.2g, Sugar: 13.4g, Protein: 2.8g

Chia Pudding

Level: Easy
Serves: 2
Preparation time: 5 minutes plus chilling time
Carbs: Moderate
Cooking time: 0 minutes

Ingredients:

- *1 cup of milk of your choice*
- *4 tablespoons chia seeds*
- *2 teaspoons maple syrup*
- *1 teaspoon vanilla extract*

To serve: Optional

- *fresh fruits of your choice*
- *nuts of your choice, chopped*
- *seeds of your choice*

Directions:

1. Combine the milk, vanilla, and maple syrup in a bowl. Add the chia seeds.
2. After 10 mins, give it a good stir and cover it in the refrigerator for 2 hours. This can be served as breakfast too.
3. Stir well. Divide the pudding into two bowls and serve with suggested options if desired.

Nutritional value per serving: Calories: 159, Fat: 8.9 g, Carbohydrates: 16.3 g, Sugar: 4.5 g, Protein: 5.4 g

HIGH-CARB RECIPES

Crispy Sweet Potatoes

Level: Easy
Serves: 2
Preparation time: 10 minutes
Carbs: High
Cooking time: 30 minutes

Ingredients:

- *1 ⅛ pounds sweet potatoes, peeled, cut into 1-inch cubes*
- *½ teaspoon ground cumin*
- *¼ teaspoon smoked paprika*
- *1 tablespoon olive oil or avocado oil*
- *½ teaspoon garlic powder*
- *Salt to taste*
- *Pepper to taste*

Directions:

1. Preheat the oven to 400 °F. Line a baking sheet with parchment paper.

2. Place the sweet potatoes in a bowl and pour the olive oil over the sweet potatoes. Toss well. Combine the salt, pepper, garlic powder, cumin, and paprika in a bowl and sprinkle all over the sweet potato cubes. Toss well.
3. Transfer the sweet potatoes onto the baking sheet. Spread the sweet potatoes evenly.
4. Bake for about 25-30 minutes. Stir the sweet potatoes halfway through baking and bake until they turn golden brown and crisp.
5. Eat with a dip of your choice.

Nutritional value per serving: Calories: 287, Fat: 7.3 g, Carbohydrates: 52.2 g, Sugar: 10.7 g, Protein: 4.3 g

---

Healthy Granola Bars

Level: Easy
Carbs: High
Serves: 5
Preparation time: 10 minutes
Cooking time: 25-30 minutes

Ingredients:

- *1 cup old-fashioned rolled oats*
- *⅛ cup sunflower seeds or pepitas*
- *¼ cup honey*
- *1 teaspoon vanilla extract*
- *⅛ teaspoon kosher salt*
- *6 tablespoons roughly chopped nuts of your choice (you can use assorted nuts)*
- *⅛ cup unsweetened coconut flakes*
- *3 tablespoons creamy peanut butter*
- *¼ teaspoon ground cinnamon*
- *3 tablespoons mini chocolate chips or dried fruits*

Directions:

1. Preheat the oven to 325 °F. Place a sheet of parchment paper in a small, square baking dish (about 6 inches) so it is overhanging from 2 sides.
2. Spray the pan with nonstick cooking spray.
3. Place the oats, coconut flakes, sunflower seeds, and nuts on a baking sheet. Do not grease the baking sheet. Spread it all over the baking sheet.
4. Place it in the oven until the coconut is light golden brown. Stir every 3-4 minutes.
5. Turn down the temperature of the oven to 300 °F.
6. In a small saucepan, combine the honey and peanut butter, and place them over medium heat. Heat, stirring often, until the mixture melts and is smooth. Turn off the heat.
7. Add the cinnamon, vanilla, and salt and mix well.
8. Add the roasted oats mixture and mix well. Cool the mixture for 6-7 minutes.
9. Stir in the chocolate chips. Ensure you do not add the chocolate chips when the mixture is hot, otherwise, the chocolate chips will melt.

10. Transfer the mixture to the baking dish and spread it evenly. Now press the mixture with the back of a glass.
11. Place it in the oven for 15-20 minutes, whether chewy or crunchy, depending on how you like it. Lesser baking time will make it chewy, and more baking time will make it crunchy.
12. Let it cool completely to room temperature. Now pick up the parchment paper with the overhanging paper and place it on your cutting board.
13. Cut into five pieces and serve. You can store them in an airtight container at room temperature for about 7-8 days or in the refrigerator for about 15 days.

Nutritional value per serving: Calories: 271, Fat: 13.4 g, Carbohydrates: 33.4 g, Sugar: 19.2 g, Protein: 7.2 g

Healthy Chocolate Pudding Snack

Level: Easy
Carbs: High
Serves: 2
Preparation time: 2 minutes
Cooking time: 0 minutes

Ingredients:

- *4 tablespoons dark cocoa powder*
- *3 tablespoons maple syrup*
- *1 cup full-fat plain Greek yogurt*

Directions:

1. Combine the yogurt, honey, and cocoa in a bowl and stir until smooth. If you find it very thick, you can dilute it with water.
2. Divide into two bowls and serve.

Nutritional value per serving: Calories: 197, Fat: 6.4 g, Carbohydrates: 30.2 g, Sugar: 21.3 g, Protein: 10.9 g

Chapter 9: Dessert and Smoothie Recipes

Low-carb Cheesecake

Level: Easy
Carbs: Low
Serves: 6
Preparation time: 20 minutes
Cooking time: 30 minutes plus chilling time

Ingredients:

- *12 ounces cream cheese at room temperature*
- *1 ¼ teaspoons pure vanilla extract*
- *⅓ cup erythritol*
- *1 cup yogurt*
- *½ tablespoon lemon juice (optional)*
- *2 tablespoons almond flour*

For the crust:

- *1 cup almond flour or pecan flour*
- *2-3 tablespoons melted coconut oil*
- *⅛ teaspoon salt*

Directions:

1. Start by preheating the oven to 350 °F.
2. To make the crust: Combine the salt, almond flour, and coconut oil in a bowl.
3. Spoon the mixture on a small springform pan (about 6 inches) and press it against the bottom. Keep it aside for now.
4. Pour enough water into a baking pan to fill up to half the pan.
5. Place the baking pan on the lowest rack in the oven.
6. Add the cream cheese, vanilla extract, erythritol, yogurt, lemon juice, and almond flour into a mixing bowl.
7. With an electric hand mixer, beat until smooth and just combined. Make sure you do not over-beat.
8. Spoon the filling over the crust. Spread it evenly. Place the springform pan on the central rack in the oven.
9. Bake for 30 minutes or until set. Don't open the oven door.
10. After cooling the cheesecake for about 20 minutes, shift the pan into the refrigerator and chill for about 8 hours.
11. Cut into six slices and serve.

Nutritional value per serving: Calories: 351.3, Fat: 34.2 g, Carbohydrates: 6.4 g, Sugar: 4.6 g, Protein: 6.7 g

Salted Caramel Cashew Fudge

Level: Easy
Serves: 12
Preparation time: 10 minutes

Carbs: Low

Cooking time: 5 minutes

Ingredients:

- *¼ cup butter*
- *½ cup swerve*
- *1 ½ teaspoons molasses*
- *½ teaspoon arrowroot powder*
- *¼ teaspoon toffee-flavored liquid stevia*
- *½ teaspoon coarse sea salt*
- *¼ cup cashew butter*
- *½ cup unsweetened cashew milk*
- *½ tablespoon maple syrup*
- *1 ¼ cups sugar-free chocolate chips*
- *⅛ cup cashew, chopped*

Directions:

1. Combine the butter and cashew butter in a saucepan. Place the saucepan over medium heat. Stir constantly until the mixture is smooth and the butter melts.
2. Add the cashew milk, maple syrup, swerve, molasses, and arrowroot powder.
3. Stir constantly until it starts boiling.
4. Turn down the heat and simmer until thick, stirring often.
5. Remove the saucepan from the heat. Add the stevia and chocolate chips.
6. Line a baking pan with parchment paper. Pour the fudge mixture into the baking pan.
7. Sprinkle the cashews and salt on top.
8. Place the pan in the refrigerator for 4-8 hours.
9. Chop into 12 equal squares and serve.

Nutritional value per serving: Calories: 153, Fat: 12.4 g, Carbohydrates: 13.9 g, Sugar: 0.84 g, Protein: 2.3 g

Avocado, Pistachio, and Green Tea Ice Cream

Level: Easy
Serves: 4
Preparation time: 10 minutes
Carbs: Low
Cooking time: 0 minutes

Ingredients:

- *¼ cup avocado oil*
- *¼ cup coconut oil*
- *1 tablespoon apple cider vinegar*
- *1 cup full-fat coconut milk*
- *½ tablespoon matcha green tea powder*
- *¼ teaspoon ground cinnamon*
- *1 large ripe Hass avocado, peeled, pitted, chopped*
- *2 egg yolks*
- *1 tablespoon gelatin*
- *1 ½ teaspoons vanilla extract*
- *⅛ teaspoon Himalayan pink salt*
- *¼ cup raw, shelled pistachios, chopped*

Directions:

1. Combine the coconut oil, egg yolks, vinegar, and avocado oil in a tall and narrow container. Let the ingredients rest for about a minute in the container.
2. Keep the immersion blender in the jar, making sure it touches the bottom of the container.
3. Turn the blender on but let it remain in a standstill position for about 20 seconds.
4. Soon the coconut oil mixture will begin to emulsify. Now you can move the blender in all directions and blend until creamy. It will look like mayonnaise.
5. Combine the gelatin, coconut milk, vanilla, matcha powder, salt, and cinnamon into another container. Blend using the immersion blender until well combined.
6. Add the blended creamy coconut oil mixture and avocado and blend until well incorporated and creamy.
7. Set up the ice cream maker following the manufacturer's instructions. Add the avocado mixture into the ice cream maker and churn the ice cream.
8. Add the pistachio nuts during the last 5 minutes of processing.
9. It is now ready to serve if you prefer soft serve consistency.
10. Spoon the ice cream into a freezer-safe container, if you like firm ice cream.
11. Freeze for about 2 hours to get slightly firm ice cream. Freezing beyond 2 hours will make the ice cream very hard.
12. If the ice cream has become very hard, thaw it in the refrigerator until the desired consistency is achieved.
13. Scoop into bowls and serve.

Nutritional value per serving: Calories: 382.4, Fat: 36.7 g, Carbohydrates: 9.7 g, Sugar: 1.46 g, Protein: 6.79 g

Blackberry and Apple Crumble

Level: Easy
Carbs: Low
Serves: 3
Preparation time: 10 minutes
Cooking time: 30 minutes

Ingredients:

For the filling:

- *¾ cup fresh or frozen blackberries*
- *2 medium zucchinis, trimmed, peeled*
- *large pinch of ground nutmeg*
- *1 teaspoon ground cinnamon*
- *1 tablespoon fresh lemon juice*
- *1 teaspoon cream of tartar*
- *3 tablespoons powdered erythritol or swerve sweetener*

For the crumble topping:

- *¾ cup almond flour*
- *1 ½ tablespoons butter or ghee or coconut oil*
- *1 tablespoon erythritol or swerve*
- *½ teaspoon vanilla bean powder or vanilla extract*

To serve: Optional

- *low-carb ice cream*
- *whipped cream*
- *yogurt*
- *coconut cream*
- *low-carb crème anglaise*

Directions:

1. Start by preheating the oven to 320 °F.
2. The zucchini will be considered as "apples." Cut the zucchini into two halves lengthwise. Scoop the seeds with a spoon and discard them. Cut the zucchini into about ¼-inch thick slices.
3. Place a pan of water over high heat. When the water starts boiling, turn the heat low and drop the zucchini slices into the simmering water.
4. Cook for a couple of minutes until slightly tender.
5. Drain in a colander. Now spread the zucchini on layers of paper towels. Dry them with paper towels.
6. Place the dried zucchini and blackberries in a baking dish. Drizzle the lemon juice on top and mix well. Sprinkle the nutmeg, cinnamon, cream of tartar, and erythritol over the blackberry mixture and mix well.
7. Place the almond flour and erythritol, if using, in a bowl. Add the vanilla and mix well.
8. Add the butter and mix using your hands until crumbly in texture.
9. Now sprinkle this mixture over the blackberry filling in the baking dish.
10. Place the baking dish in the oven to bake until golden brown on top, for about 30 minutes.
11. Remove the baking dish and allow it to cool for about 10 minutes.
12. Serve with any of the suggested serving options if desired.

Nutritional value per serving: Calories: 238.9, Fat: 19.43 g, Carbs: 13.11 g, Sugar: 6.32 g, Protein: 7.12 g

Lemon Coconut Custard Pie

Level: Easy
Serves: 4
Preparation time: 10 minutes

Carbs: Low

Cooking time: 45 minutes

Ingredients:

- *1 large egg*
- *6 tablespoons erythritol*
- *1 tablespoon unsalted butter, melted, cooled*
- *¼ + ⅛ teaspoon baking powder*
- *¼ teaspoon lemon extract*
- *½ cup canned coconut milk*
- *2 tablespoons coconut flour*
- *½ teaspoon vanilla extract*
- *½ teaspoon grated lemon zest*
- *2 ounces of unsweetened coconut*

Directions:

1. Grease a 6-inch pie pan with cooking spray.
2. Add the eggs, sweetener, butter, vanilla, lemon extract, lemon zest, coconut milk, coconut flour, and baking powder into a mixing bowl and mix until just incorporated.
3. Add the unsweetened coconut and fold gently.
4. Transfer into the prepared pie pan.
5. Preheat the oven to 350 °F.
6. Bake until light golden brown on top, it should take 30 minutes.
7. Cool completely. Cut into 4 equal slices and serve.

Nutritional value per serving: Calories: 208.9, Fat: 19.3 g, Carbohydrates: 5.8 g, Sugar: 0.9 g, Protein: 2.7 g

Pineapple Cream

Level: Easy
Serves: 3
Preparation time: 5 minutes

Carbs: Low

Cooking time: 0 minutes

Ingredients:

- *8 ounces frozen pineapple chunks*
- *½ tablespoon lemon juice or lime juice*
- *½ cup frozen mango chunks*

Directions:

1. Place the frozen mango, pineapple, and lemon juice in the food processor bowl and process until smooth.

Nutritional value per serving: Calories: 57, Fat: 0 g, Carbs: 13.4 g, Sugar: 12.1 g, Protein: 1 g

Vegan Cucumber Green Smoothie

Level: Easy
Serves: 1
Preparation time: 5 minutes

Carbs: Low

Cooking time: 0 minutes

Ingredients:

- *½ inch ginger, peeled, sliced*
- *juice of ½ lemon*
- *⅓ cup cold water*
- *¼ cup chopped cilantro*
- *¾ cup sliced cucumber*
- *½ cup frozen or fresh avocado*
- *a pinch of Himalayan pink salt*

Directions:

1. Place the ginger, Himalayan pink salt, lemon juice, cold water, cilantro, cucumber, and avocado in a blender.
2. Blend until you get a smooth mixture.
3. Pour into a glass and serve.

Nutritional value per serving: Calories: 147.8, Fat: 9.9 g, Carbohydrates: 13.6 g, Sugar: 6.7 g, Protein: 1.8 g

---

Minty Green Smoothie

Level: Easy
Serves: 2
Preparation time: 5 minutes

Carbs: Low

Cooking time: 0 minutes

Ingredients:

- *1 avocado, peeled, pitted, and chopped*
- *2 cups fresh spinach*
- *stevia drops to taste (optional)*
- *1 cup unsweetened almond milk*
- *ice cubes, as required*
- *2 scoops whey protein powder*
- *½ teaspoon peppermint extract*
- *cacao nibs to garnish (optional)*

Directions:

1. Blend the avocado, protein powder, spinach, stevia drops, and milk until you get a smooth puree.
2. Add ice cubes and blend until very chilled.
3. Pour into two glasses and serve.

Nutritional value per serving: Calories: 293.2, Fat: 14.5 g, Carbohydrates: 10.8 g, Sugar: 1.3 g, Protein: 29.8 g

Healthy Carrot Cake

Level: Easy
Carbs: Moderate
Serves: 24
Preparation time: 20 minutes
Cooking time: 60-70 minutes

Ingredients:

- *1 cup Greek extra-virgin olive oil*
- *2/3 cup 2% low-fat milk*
- *6 eggs at room temperature*
- *1 cup low-fat Greek yogurt*
- *1 cup dark honey*
- *4 ½ cups whole-wheat flour*
- *1 teaspoon salt*
- *3 teaspoons baking powder*
- *8 teaspoons ground cinnamon*
- *½ teaspoon ground ginger*
- *1 teaspoon ground cardamom*
- *4 cups finely grated carrots*
- *2/3 cup chopped walnuts*
- *12 medjool dates, pitted, finely chopped*
- *powdered sugar to dust*

Directions:

1. Preheat the oven to 350 °F. Grease a large baking dish with cooking oil spray. Place a sheet of parchment paper as well.
2. Add the Greek yogurt, olive oil, and milk into a bowl and whisk well.
3. Add the eggs, one at a time, and whisk until well incorporated.
4. Add the whole-wheat flour, salt, baking powder, cinnamon, and ginger into a mixing bowl and stir until well combined.
5. Add the flour mixture into the bowl of egg mixture and stir until well combined.
6. Add the carrots and fold gently. Sprinkle the dates and walnuts all over the batter and stir until well combined.
7. Spoon the batter into the prepared baking dish and pop it into the oven.
8. Set the timer for an hour and bake until cooked through. To check if it is cooked through, do a toothpick test. Check if any batter is stuck on the toothpick. If you find any batter, you will need to bake it for 5-7 minutes longer.
9. Take out the baking dish from the oven and let it cool for a few minutes in the dish itself.
10. Invert onto a plate. Peel off the parchment paper. Cut into 24 squares and serve.
11. Place the extra cake in an airtight container in the refrigerator. They can last for 8-10 days. You can freeze them for about a month.

Nutritional value per serving: Calories: 167.8, Fat: 8.36 g, Carbohydrates: 19.3 g, Sugar: 9.79 g, Protein: 6.3 g

Oatmeal Cookies

Level: Easy
Serves: 32
Preparation time: 10 minutes

Carbs: Moderate

Cooking time: 10 minutes

Ingredients:

- *2/3 cup honey or maple syrup or agave nectar*
- *2 large eggs*
- *½ cup coconut oil or unsalted butter melted*
- *2 teaspoons vanilla extract*
- *1 cup whole-wheat flour*
- *2 teaspoons ground cinnamon*
- *2 cups instant oats*
- *2 teaspoons baking powder*
- *½ teaspoon salt*
- *½ cup raisins or cranberries*
- *½ cup chocolate chips (optional)*

Directions:

1. Start by preheating the oven to 350 °F. Place a sheet of parchment paper on a large baking sheet.
2. Crack the eggs into a bowl. Add the honey, vanilla, and coconut oil and whisk until well combined.
3. Combine the whole-wheat flour, cinnamon, oats, baking powder, and salt in a bowl.
4. Add the flour mixture into the bowl of egg mixture and stir until well combined.
5. Using a cookie scoop, scoop out the dough and place it on the baking sheet. Place as many as can fit on the sheet but make sure to leave a sufficient gap between them. The remaining cookies can be baked in batches.
6. Place the baking sheet in the oven to bake with the timer set for 10 minutes.
7. Rest the cookies on the baking sheet for 5-8 minutes. Loosen the cookies by sliding a metal spatula under the cookies. Now place them on a wire rack to cool completely.
8. Store the cookies in an airtight container. They can last for 7-10 days at room temperature.

Nutritional value per serving: Calories: 143.7, Fat: 4.8 g, Carbohydrates: 21.2 g, Sugar: 7.8 g, Protein: 3.2 g

Pumpkin Cheesecake Cups

Level: Easy
Carbs: Moderate
Serves: 4
Preparation time: 25 minutes
Cooking time: 5 minutes

Ingredients:

For the pecan topping:

- *3 tablespoons pecans*
- *⅛ teaspoon pumpkin pie spice*
- *1 graham cracker, break into 1-inch pieces*

For cheesecake mousse:

- *3 ounces cream cheese, at room temperature, cut into 1-inch cubes*
- *2 tablespoons pure maple syrup or honey*
- *¼ cup thick, full-fat plain yogurt or Greek yogurt*
- *½ teaspoon vanilla extract*

For the pumpkin mousse:

- *¼ cup thick, full-fat plain yogurt or Greek yogurt*
- *2 tablespoons pure maple syrup or honey*
- *⅛ teaspoon vanilla extract*
- *½ can (from a 15-ounce can) of pumpkin puree*
- *1-ounce cream cheese at room temperature*
- *½ tablespoon pumpkin pie spice*
- *tiny pinch of salt*

Directions:

1. To make pecan topping: Place the pecans in a small skillet. Place the skillet over medium heat and toast for about 3 minutes or until you get a nice aroma. Stir often.
2. Turn off the heat and add them to the food processor bowl. Add the graham cracker pieces and give short pulses until they break into small pieces.
3. Remove the mixture into a bowl. Take a clean kitchen towel and wipe the food processor bowl.
4. To make cheesecake mousse: Place the cream cheese, maple syrup, yogurt, and vanilla extract in the food processor bowl.
5. Next, prepare the pumpkin mousse: Add the pumpkin puree, cream cheese, pumpkin pie spice, salt, yogurt, maple syrup, and vanilla into the food processor bowl.
6. Process until very smooth. Scrape the sides of the bowl whenever required.
7. Remove the blended mixture into another bowl.
8. To assemble the cheesecake cups: Divide the pumpkin mousse equally into four cups.
9. Divide the cheesecake mousse equally and place it over the pumpkin mousse.
10. Divide the pecan mixture equally and place it over the cheesecake mousse layer.
11. If you like the dessert at room temperature, you can serve it right away or chill and serve it later.
12. To serve later: Cover each cup with cling wrap and place it in the refrigerator. They can last for 2 days.

Nutritional value per serving: Calories: 272.3, Fat: 16.6 g, Carbohydrates: 28.6 g, Sugar: 18.4, Protein: 6.3 g

Strawberry Banana Smoothie

Level: Easy
Serves: 1
Preparation time: 5 minutes

Carbs: Moderate

Cooking time: 0 minutes

Ingredients:

- *1 cup frozen strawberries*
- *½ cup almond milk or any milk of your choice*
- *½ medium banana, sliced*
- *¼ cup plain Greek yogurt (optional)*

Directions:

1. Place the strawberries, milk, banana, and Greek yogurt, if using, in a blender.
2. Blend until you get a smooth puree.
3. Pour into a glass and serve.

Nutritional value per serving: Calories: 119.2, Fat: 1.7 g, Carbohydrates: 25.6 g, Sugar: 14.6 g, Protein: 2.1 g

Vegan Mango Chia Seed Smoothie

Level: Easy
Serves: 2
Preparation time: 2 minutes

Carbs: High

Cooking time: 0 minutes

Ingredients:

- *2 cups frozen mango pieces*
- *½ cup vegan yogurt*
- *liquid stevia or monk fruit sweetener to taste (optional)*
- *2 cups almond milk*
- *2 tablespoons chia seeds*

Directions:

1. Blend the mango, yogurt, sweetener, almond milk, and chia seeds in a blender until you get a smooth puree.
2. Divide the smoothie into two glasses and serve.

Nutritional value per serving: Calories: 206.7, Fat: 8.12 g, Carbohydrates: 28.67 g, Sugar: 19.23 g, Protein: 4.12 g

Berry Crisp

Level: Easy
Carbs: High
Serves: 5
Preparation time: 10 minutes
Cooking time: 40 minutes

Ingredients:

For the filling:

- *2 cups blueberries, fresh or frozen (thawed if frozen)*
- *1 cup blackberries, fresh or frozen (thawed if frozen)*
- *1 cup raspberries*
- *2 tablespoons pure maple syrup*
- *juice of ½ lemon*

For the topping:

- *½ cup oat flour*
- *⅛ teaspoon salt*
- *¼ cup chopped pecans (optional)*
- *4 tablespoons pure maple syrup*
- *½ cup whole rolled oats*
- *¼ teaspoon ground cinnamon*
- *3 tablespoons melted, refined coconut oil*

Directions:

1. Firstly, preheat the oven to 350 °F.
2. To make the filling: Combine the blackberries, blueberries, and raspberries in a baking dish (about 6-7 inches). Add maple syrup and lemon juice and mix well.
3. To make the topping: Add the oat flour, salt, pecans, cinnamon, and rolled oats into a bowl and mix well.
4. Mix in the maple syrup and coconut oil. Let the topping rest for a couple of minutes.
5. Scatter the mixture over the berry filling. Do not cover the baking dish.
6. Place the baking dish in the oven and set the timer for about 40 minutes or until golden brown.
7. Once baked, take out the baking dish and allow it to cool for about 15 minutes.

Nutritional value per serving: Calories: 304.8, Fat: 12.3 g, Carbohydrates: 46.6 g, Sugar: 22.1 g, Protein: 4.5 g

Chocolate Avocado Mousse

Level: Easy
Carbs: High
Serves: 4
Preparation time: 10 minutes
Cooking time: 0 minutes

Ingredients:

- *4 medium ripe avocados, peeled, pitted, chopped*
- *2 tablespoons vanilla extract*
- *2 teaspoons ground cinnamon*
- *4 tablespoons of coconut nectar or agave nectar*
- *4-6 tablespoons unsweetened almond milk, if required*
- *6 tablespoons cacao powder*

Directions:

1. Place the avocado, vanilla, cinnamon, cacao powder, and sweetener in a blender and blend until smooth.
2. If you want fluffy mousse, add a little almond milk while blending.
3. Scoop into four bowls and serve.

Nutritional value per serving: Calories: 471, Fat: 33 g, Carbohydrates: 36.7 g, Sugar: 11.3 g, Protein: 8.9 g

Key Lime Pie Smoothie

Level: Easy
Carbs: High
Serves: 2
Preparation time: 5 minutes
Cooking time: 0 minutes

Ingredients:

- *2 bananas, sliced, frozen*
- *½ cup key lime juice or regular lime juice*
- *1 teaspoon finely grated lime zest*
- *ice cubes, as required (optional)*
- *1 cup plain Greek yogurt*
- *2 tablespoons honey*
- *½ teaspoon vanilla extract*
- *a large handful of fresh spinach leaves (optional)*

Directions:

1. Place the frozen banana slices, lime juice, zest, yogurt, honey, and vanilla extract into a blender.
2. Add the spinach and ice cubes if using, and blend the mixture until smooth.
3. Distribute the smoothie into two glasses and serve.

Nutritional value per serving: Calories: 253.2, Fat: 0.7 g, Carbohydrates: 54.3 g, Sugar: 36.8 g, Protein: 11.6 g

Chocolate Strawberry Smoothie

Level: Easy
Carbs: High
Serves: 1
Preparation time: 5 minutes
Cooking time: 0 minutes

Ingredients:

- *½ cup frozen strawberries*
- *¼ cup old-fashioned oats*
- *½ tablespoon almond butter*
- *1 tablespoon maple syrup or honey*
- *½ tablespoon chopped dark chocolate to garnish*
- *½ banana, sliced*
- *2 tablespoons cocoa powder*
- *6 tablespoons milk of your preference*
- *ice cubes as required*

Directions:

1. Add the strawberries, oats, almond butter, maple syrup, banana, cocoa powder, milk, and ice cubes into a blender.
2. Blend until very smooth.
3. Pour into a glass and serve garnished with a sprinkle of chopped dark chocolate.

Nutritional value per serving: Calories: 321.3, Fat: 6.3 g, Carbohydrates: 59.6 g, Sugar: 27.8 g, Protein: 10.5 g

Banana Peach Smoothie

Level: Easy
Carbs: High
Serves: 1
Preparation time: 5 minutes
Cooking time: 0 minutes

Ingredients:

- *1 cup sliced frozen peaches*
- *4-6 tablespoons pure orange juice*
- *Ice cubes, as required*
- *½ tablespoon vanilla protein powder (optional)*
- *½ large banana, sliced*
- *Water or required*
- *¼ teaspoon vanilla extract*

Directions:

1. Add the banana, peaches, orange juice, ice cubes, protein powder, water, and vanilla extract into a blender and blend until smooth.
2. Pour into a glass and serve.

Nutritional value per serving: Calories: 173.4, Fat: 0.9 g, Carbohydrates: 38.7 g, Sugar: 25.4 g, Protein: 6.8 g

Low Fat Tropical Layered Smoothie

Level: Moderate
Carbs: High
Serves: 1
Preparation time: 15 minutes
Cooking time: 0 minutes

Ingredients:

For the 1st layer:

- *¼ cup low-fat plain Greek yogurt*
- *¼ cup frozen mango chunks*
- *¼ cup frozen blueberries*
- *½ tablespoon fresh lemon juice*
- *1 tablespoon agave nectar*

For the 2nd layer:

- *¼ cup plain Greek yogurt*
- *½ tablespoon fresh lemon juice*
- *½ small banana, peeled, sliced*
- *1 tablespoon agave nectar*
- *¼ cup frozen mango*

For the 3rd layer:

- *¼ cup plain Greek yogurt*
- *½ small banana, peeled, sliced*
- *½ tablespoon fresh lemon juice*
- *½ cup frozen strawberries*
- *1 tablespoon agave nectar*

For toppings: Optional

- *blueberries*
- *pomegranate arils*

Directions:

1. For the 1st layer: Add the yogurt, mango, blueberries, lemon juice, and agave nectar into a blender. Blend until very smooth and thick.
2. Pour the smoothie into a glass. Place the glass in the freezer. Wash the blender.
3. For the 2nd layer: Add the mango, Greek yogurt, lemon juice, banana, and agave nectar into a blender. Blend until very smooth and thick.
4. Gently pour the smoothie over the 1st layer. Place the glass in the freezer.
5. Wash the blender.
6. For the 3rd layer: Add the Greek yogurt, banana, lemon juice, strawberries, and agave nectar into the blender. Blend until very smooth and thick.
7. Pour the smoothie gently over the 2nd layer. Place the glass in the freezer for 8 to 10 minutes.
8. Top with suggested topping and serve.

Nutritional value per serving: Calories: 571, Fat: 3.4 g, Carbohydrates: 121.3 g, Sugar: 91.2 g, Protein: 22.7 g

Smoothie Bowl

Level: Easy
Serves: 2
Preparation time: 5 minutes

Carbs: High

Cooking time: 0 minutes

Ingredients:

- *2 peeled, frozen bananas*
- *1 cup chocolate milk*
- *1 cup milk*
- *⅛ cup natural peanut butter*
- *½ teaspoon ground cinnamon*
- *1 cup original Cheerios*
- *⅛ cup flaxseed meal*

For toppings: Choose any

- *Banana slices*
- *Chocolate chips*
- *Cheerios*
- *Flaxseeds*
- *Cacao nibs*
- *Shredded coconut*
- *Peanut butter*

Directions:

1. Place the bananas, chocolate milk, milk, peanut butter, cinnamon, cheerios, and flaxseed meal in a blender and blend until smooth. You can use dairy or nondairy milk of your choice.
2. Divide into two bowls. Place the desired toppings on top and serve.

Nutritional value per serving: Calories: 458.9, Fat: 19.7 g, Carbohydrates: 61.2 g, Sugar: 38.9, Protein: 17.1 g

Chapter 10: 30-Day Meal Plan

In this chapter, we will look at a basic 30-days meal plan for people who would like to follow carb cycling for overall health benefits and weight loss.

While following the meal plan, try to incorporate some daily exercises in your routine. This is essential if you want to lose weight and reap the other benefits of the diet.

You can choose to rest on low-carb days. On days you consume minimal carbs, your energy levels will be lower, and it is better not to overexert yourself.

However, the high-carb days should ideally include some cardio or aerobic exercise so you can burn off any excess calories.

A good rule of thumb is to avoid reducing calories per day below 1500 if you are moderately active. A diet below this number can cause sluggishness and hunger pangs, and overall slows your metabolism.

Day# 1 - Monday - High-Carb (about 200g)

Breakfast: Healthy pancakes
Lunch: Turkey sandwich
Dinner: Black bean fajita skillet
Snack: Crispy sweet potatoes
Dessert: Berry crisp
Exercise: Weight Training

Day# 2 - Tuesday - Moderate-Carb (about 100g)

Breakfast: Bagel avocado toast
Lunch: Asian lettuce wraps
Dinner: Ground beef tacos
Snack: Spicy mixed nuts
Dessert: Salted caramel cashew fudge
Exercise: Aerobic Exercise

Day# 3 - Wednesday - Low-Carb (about 30g)

Breakfast: Veggie scrambled eggs
Lunch: Chicken and white bean soup
Dinner: Sage-rubbed salmon
Snack: Mini cheese balls
Dessert: Low-carb Cheesecake
Rest Day

Day# 4 - Thursday - High-Carb (about 200g)

Breakfast: Brownie batter oatmeal
Lunch: Quick quesadilla
Dinner: Vegan burrito bowls
Snack: Trail mix
Dessert: Oatmeal cookies
Exercise: Weight Training

Day# 5 - Friday - Moderate-Carb (about 100g)

Breakfast: Cottage cheese bowl
Lunch: Kale and Brussels sprouts salad
Dinner: Ground turkey skillet
Snack: Buffalo chicken wings
Dessert: Blackberry and apple crumble
Exercise: Aerobic Exercises

Day# 6 - Saturday - Low-Carb (about 30g)

Breakfast: Omelet muffins
Lunch: Shrimp cauliflower gnocchi
Dinner: Chicken parmesan
Snack: Caprese salad kabobs
Rest Day

Day# 7 - Sunday - Low-Carb (about 30g)

Breakfast: Spinach enchilada omelet
Lunch: Buffalo chicken salad
Dinner: Mediterranean chicken
Snack: Mini cheese balls
Rest Day

Day# 8 - Monday - High-Carb (about 200g)

Breakfast: Banana waffles
Lunch: Greek pita pockets
Dinner: Meatloaf + mashed sweet potatoes
Snack: Minty green smoothie
Dessert: Healthy carrot cake
Exercise: Weight Training

Day# 9 - Tuesday - Moderate-Carb (about 100g)

Breakfast: Yogurt bowl
Lunch: Grilled chicken
Dinner: Spicy grilled eggplant
Snack: Tortilla rolls
Dessert: Avocado, pistachio, and green tea ice cream
Exercise: Aerobic Exercises

Day# 10 - Wednesday - Low-Carb (about 30g)

Breakfast: Parmesan spinach cakes
Lunch: Chipotle-orange broccoli tofu
Dinner: Parmesan roasted broccoli
Snack: Spicy lemon chicken kabobs
Rest Day

Day# 11 - Thursday - High-Carb (about 200g)

Breakfast: Oatmeal with tofu
Lunch: Grilled veggie pizza
Dinner: Couscous with shrimp and peas
Snack: Chia pudding
Dessert: Oatmeal cookies
Exercise: Weight Training

Day# 12 - Friday - Moderate-Carb (about 100g)

Breakfast: Southwest tortilla scramble
Lunch: Chicken soup with vegetables
Dinner: Poached salmon with cucumber
Snack: Healthy granola bars
Dessert: Blackberry and apple crumble
Exercise: Aerobic Exercises

Day# 13 - Saturday - Low-Carb (about 30g)

Breakfast: Smoked salmon and cream cheese omelet
Lunch: Vegetable soup
Dinner: Baked salsa chicken
Snack: Savory date and pistachio bites
Dessert: Low-carb cheesecake
Rest Day

Day# 14 - Sunday - Low-Carb (about 30g)

Breakfast: Veggie scrambled eggs
Lunch: Chicken cobb salad
Dinner: Parmesan baked cod
Snack: Mini cheese balls
Dessert: Blackberry and apple crumble
Rest Day

Day# 15 - Monday - High-Carb (about 200g)

Breakfast: Vegan dark chocolate quinoa bowl
Lunch: Apple and spinach salad with honey balsamic vinaigrette
Dinner: Spaghetti with Spinach Pesto
Snack: Banana peach smoothie
Dessert: Berry crisp
Exercise: Weight Training

Day# 16 - Tuesday - Moderate-Carb (about 100g)

Breakfast: Veggie hash
Lunch: Cajun shrimp and sausage vegetable skillet
Dinner: Lemon-broccoli pasta with parmesan
Snack: Trail mix
Dessert: Avocado, pistachio, and green tea ice cream
Exercise: Aerobic Exercises

Day# 17 - Wednesday - Low-Carb (about 30g)

Breakfast: Avocado egg tarts
Lunch: Minty watermelon cucumber salad
Dinner: Golden apricot-glazed turkey breast
Snack: Buffalo chicken wings
Rest Day

Day# 18 - Thursday - High-Carb (about 200g)

Breakfast: Berry yogurt breakfast parfait
Lunch: Vegan sandwich
Dinner: Chicken and vegetable curry couscous
Snack: Healthy Granola Bars
Dessert: Chocolate strawberry smoothie
Exercise: Weight Training

Day# 19 - Friday - Moderate-Carb (about 100g)

Breakfast: Baked French toast casserole
Lunch: Chicken Cobb salad
Dinner: Pasta with tuna
Snack: Peanut butter energy balls
Exercise: Aerobic Exercises

Day# 20 - Saturday - Low-Carb (about 30g)

Breakfast: Egg muffin cups
Lunch: Cod and asparagus bake
Dinner: Baked salsa chicken
Snack: Spicy mixed nuts
Rest Day

Day# 21 - Sunday - Low-Carb (about 30g)

Breakfast: Veggie scrambled eggs
Lunch: Chicken and white bean soup
Dinner: Sage-rubbed salmon
Snack: Mini cheese balls
Rest Day

Day# 22 - Monday - High-Carb (about 200g)

Breakfast: Vegan omelet
Lunch: Sweet potato and cauliflower rice bowl
Dinner: Chickpea tortilla soup
Snack: Healthy chocolate pudding snack
Dessert: Oatmeal cookies
Exercise: Weight Training

Day# 23 - Tuesday - Moderate-Carb (about 100g)

Breakfast: Vegan superfood breakfast bowl
Lunch: Buffalo chicken salad
Dinner: Linguine skillet
Snack: Savory date and pistachio bites
Dessert: Low-carb cheesecake
Exercise: Aerobic Exercises

Day# 24 - Wednesday - Low-Carb (about 30g)

Breakfast: Yogurt pancakes
Lunch: Cod and asparagus bake
Dinner: Turkey chili
Snack: Caprese salad kabobs
Rest Day

Day# 25 - Thursday - High-Carb (about 200g)

Breakfast: Blueberry baked oatmeal
Lunch: Hearty chickpea and spinach stew
Dinner: Goat cheese and broccoli pasta
Snack: Fruit kabobs with cream cheese dip
Dessert: Berry crisp
Exercise: Weight Training

Day# 26 - Friday - Moderate-Carb (about 100g)

Breakfast: Ricotta and yogurt parfait
Lunch: White bean and veggie salad
Dinner: Warm chicken salad with peas and polenta
Snack: Chia pudding
Exercise: Aerobic Exercises

Day# 27 - Saturday - Low-Carb (about 30g)

Breakfast: Omelet muffins
Lunch: Chicken and white bean soup
Dinner: Baked salsa chicken
Snack: Lemon coconut custard pie
Rest Day

Day# 28 - Sunday - Low-Carb (about 30g)

Breakfast: Smoked salmon and cream cheese omelet
Lunch: Vegetable soup
Dinner: Golden apricot-glazed turkey breast
Snack: Savory date and pistachio bites
Rest Day

Day# 29 - Monday - High-Carb (about 200g)

Breakfast: Chocolate strawberry smoothie
Lunch: Farro salad
Dinner: One pot of ground turkey pasta
Snack: Banana and chocolate mini muffins
Dessert: Key lime pie smoothie
Exercise: Weight Training

Day# 30 - Tuesday - Moderate-Carb (about 100g)

Breakfast: Parmesan spinach cakes
Lunch: Asian lettuce wraps
Dinner: Chicken pesto rolls
Snack: Tortilla rolls
Dessert: Healthy carrot cake
Exercise: Aerobic Exercises

Conversion Tables

COOKING CONVERSION CHART

WEIGHT

IMPERIAL	METRIC
1/2 oz	15 g
1 oz	29 g
2 oz	57 g
3 oz	85 g
4 oz	113 g
5 oz	141 g
6 oz	170 g
8 oz	227 g
10 oz	283 g
12 oz	340 g
13 oz	369 g
14 oz	397 g
15 oz	425 g
1 lb	453 g

TEMPERATURE

FAHRENHEIT	CELSIUS
100 °F	37 °C
150 °F	65 °C
200 °F	93 °C
250 °F	121 °C
300 °F	150 °C
325 °F	160 °C
350 °F	180 °C
375 °F	190 °C
400 °F	200 °C
425 °F	220 °C
450 °F	230 °C
500 °F	260 °C
525 °F	274 °C
550 °F	288 °C

MEASUREMENT

CUP	ONCES	MILLILITERS	TBSP
8 cup	64 oz	1895 ml	128
6 cup	48 oz	1420 ml	96
5 cup	40 oz	1180 ml	80
4 cup	32 oz	960 ml	64
2 cup	16 oz	500 ml	32
1 cup	8 oz	250 ml	16
3/4 cup	6 oz	177 ml	12
2/3 cup	5 oz	158 ml	11
1/2 cup	4 oz	118 ml	8
3/8 cup	3 oz	90 ml	6
1/3 cup	2.5 oz	79 ml	5.5
1/4 cup	2 oz	59 ml	4
1/8 cup	1 oz	30 ml	3
1/16 cup	1/2 oz	15 ml	1

Index

Conclusion

Carb cycling is a very effective and safe diet that has multiple benefits. This approach to alternating carbohydrate amounts helps in conditioning your body to become more efficient in burning carbs and fats. Following low-carb or no-carb diets is not feasible over the long-term and does not work as well as this diet.

With the carb cycle meal plan, you can achieve all your goals regardless of age, gender, or lifestyle, if you combine it with regular exercise. Carb cycling will help boost weight loss and reduce body fat percentage. Your muscle mass will increase, and muscle wasting can be prevented. When following other diets, you might lose unhealthy amounts of muscle or weaken the muscle tissue.

Rebuilding and repairing muscle tissue is difficult unless you eat right and exercise regularly. This can be achieved with carb cycling. The exercises provided in this book will also help you improve your overall flexibility, stability, and strength in conjunction with the diet. You will also notice an increase in your energy levels and fewer hormonal imbalances. Your hunger pangs will be curbed, and it will become easier to eat healthier.

All the recipes in the book are compatible with the carb cycling diet. Use the shopping list as a guide to stocking up your pantry and cooking healthy meals supporting your health goals. There is also a 30-days meal plan So, if you are ready to benefit from carb cycling, start implementing the guidelines and get cooking.

References

Anconitano, V. (n.d.). *Carb cycling diet beginners' guide for 2023*. Thefoodellers. https://thefoodellers.com/en/carb cycling-diet

Braverman, J. (2018, December 29). *How many carbs should you have on a low carb diet?* Livestrong. https://www.livestrong.com/article/265196-how-many-carbs-do-you-need-on-a-low-carb-diet/

Cyklopedia. (2019, November 23). *Carb cycling | One week meal plan with shopping list*. Cyklopedia. https://cyklopedia.cc/cycling-nutrition/carb cycling-meal-plan/

Illustrated Exercise Guide. (2017). Spotebi. https://www.spotebi.com/exercise-guide/

Kamb, S. (2020, March 17). *Bodyweight workout for beginners: 20-minute at home routine* | Nerd Fitness. https://www.nerdfitness.com/blog/beginner-body-weight-workout-burn-fat-build-muscle/

Levy, J. (2023, March 27). *Carb cycling diet: The missing part of your weight loss plan?* Dr. Axe. https://draxe.com/nutrition/carb cycling-diet/

McGrane, K. (2022, March 31). *14 healthy high fiber, low carb foods*. Healthline. https://www.healthline.com/nutrition/high-fiber-low-carb-foods#1.-Flax-seeds

Metabolic Meals. (2021, June 20). *Carb cycling: The 30-day nutrition plan that actually works*. Metabolic Meals. https://blog.mymetabolicmeals.com/carb cycling-the-30-day-nutrition-plan-that-actually-works/

Pritzker, S. (2020, December 11). *Carb cycling meal plan for fat loss*. Oxygen Mag. https://www.oxygenmag.com/nutrition-for-women/nutrition-tips-for-women/carb cycling-for-fat-loss/

Made in United States
North Haven, CT
10 September 2023

41381833R00083